I0135995

Teaching and Learning Creatively

About the Editors

All the editors are at Clemson University and have been with the project since its inception in 2000. Patti Connor-Greene teaches psychology courses including Abnormal Psychology, The Social Construction of Madness, Psychology and Culture, and Women and Psychology. Catherine Mobley teaches sociology courses including Introductory Sociology, Policy and Social Change, Field Placement, and Evaluation Research. Catherine Paul teaches humanities and English courses including Modern Fiction and Poetry and Museums in Modern Culture. Jerry Waldvogel teaches biology courses including General Biology, Evolution and Creationism, and Field Methods in Ecology and Behavior. Art Young teaches English courses including Advanced Writing and Nineteenth Century British Literature. Managing Editor Liz Wright is a Master of Arts in Professional Communication student and graduate research assistant to the Robert S. Campbell Chair in Technical Communication.

www.ingramcontent.com/pod-product-compliance
Lightning Source LLC
Chambersburg PA
CBHW050353100426
42739CB00015BB/3384

9 781932 559828

Teaching and Learning Creatively

Inspirations and Reflections

Edited by

Patricia A. Connor-Greene, Catherine Mobley, Catherine E. Paul, Jerry A. Waldvogel, and Art Young

Managing Editor: Liz Wright

Parlor Press
West Lafayette, Indiana
www.parlorpress.com

Parlor Press LLC, West Lafayette, Indiana 47906

© 2006 by Parlor Press
All rights reserved.

Printed in the United States of America
S A N: 2 5 4—8 8 7 9

Library of Congress Cataloging-in-Publication Data

Teaching and learning creatively : inspirations and reflections / edited
by Patricia A. Connor-Greene, Catherine Mobley, Catherine E. Paul, Jerry
A. Waldvogel, and Art Young ; managing editor, Liz Wright.
        p. cm.
    ISBN 1-932559-82-5 (pbk. : alk. paper) -- ISBN 1-932559-83-3
(hardcover : alk. paper) -- ISBN 1-932559-84-1 (adobe ebook) 1. College
students' writings, American--South Carolina--Clemson. 2. American
poetry--21st century. 3. American poetry--South Carolina--Clemson. 4.
Clemson University. I. Connor-Greene, Patricia A. II. Clemson University.
    PS591.C65T43 2006
    810.8'0928309757--dc22
                                    2006007228

Cover image: "Children's Water Garden" by Renee Keydoszius
Cover design by Liz Wright
Printed on acid-free paper.

Parlor Press, LLC is an independent publisher of scholarly and trade titles in
print and multimedia formats. This book is available in paperback and Adobe
eBook formats from Parlor Press on the WWW at http://www.parlorpress.com.
For submission information or to find out about Parlor Press publications, write
to Parlor Press, 816 Robinson St., West Lafayette, Indiana, 47906, or e-mail
editor@parlorpress.com.

Contents

Contents

CONTENTS

Contents

Contents

CONTENTS

Acknowledgments

Thank you to our numerous colleagues and the thousands of students who have participated in the Teaching and Learning Creatively project, particularly those students and teachers who are represented in this collection. Our projects have been sponsored by the R. Roy and Marnie Pearce Center for Professional Communication and the Robert S. Campbell Chair Endowment at Clemson University, and we are grateful for their generous support. We thank the editors and authors of the book that inspired us to create this one: *Teaching with Fire: Poetry That Sustains the Courage to Teach,* editors Sam M. Intrator and Megan Scribner (San Francisco: Jossey-Bass, 2003). The editors want especially to thank our Managing Editor, Liz Wright, for her invaluable role in conceiving, planning, organizing, and publishing this book.

Six of the student poems presented in this volume first appeared in *Language and Learning Across the Disciplines* (June 2003, Volume 6, No. 2, available online at the WAC Clearinghouse http://wac.colostate.edu/), in a special issue on "Poetry Across the Curriculum." We thank the editor of *LLAD,* Sharon Quiroz, for permission to publish them in this collection. The poems are:

    "Mental Health Professional," by Laurie Gambrell

    "Nude Descending a Staircase," by Jason Snelgrove

    "Fertilization Poem," by Maureen McHugh

    "Ode to Math," by Maureen McHugh

    "I watch those hands . . . ," by Amanda Oberdorff

    "Region of Rejection: Gettysburg Address Revised," by Bo Gillooly

Reading This Book

This collection offers a glimpse into the Teaching and Learning Creatively project at Clemson University. The project began with assignments of poetry writing in courses across the curriculum and grew to include other kinds of creative responses. We offer here a smattering of the work produced to date under these projects. Many of the visual works were first produced in color. If you are interested in seeing the original color images, or would like to find more examples of creative works and links to further reading, please consult our website http://people. clemson.edu/~apyoung/projects/tlc/book.html.

Each example of student work is accompanied by a reflection from the teacher who made the assignment. The pairings show something of the student-teacher interaction that has happened because of this project. Teachers tell you why they think their students' work demonstrates a richer understanding of course material or a surprising burst of imagination, and as often as not, they tell you something they learned from that student.

You can read this book as a series of examples of the kind of work and play that can come from this cross-disciplinary project. You can also read these students' creative responses to academic learning as a representation of the complex webs of teaching and learning in modern classrooms, where teachers learn and learners teach. From the collection presented here, other teachers might be inspired to experiment in their own classrooms, to find new ways of hearing from and listening to their students.

And we are certain you will find ways of reading this volume that we have not even considered, for that is truly the nature of teaching and learning creatively.

Teaching and Writing Creatively

The Challenge of Teaching Creatively

As teachers, we have all spent time poring over student work—papers, lab-books, exams, problem sets, design projects, artworks. We have slogged through the mundane (and the ridiculous), reveled in the surprising, celebrated the excellent, and even sat back to admire growth beyond all expectations, patting ourselves gently on the back even as we praise our students. But there is a rare pleasure that comes in encountering our students' voices in unusual venues. When we see a student performing in a play, her voice becoming something other than her own; we are surprised to find those sentiments, those experiences coming from that mouth. Or we hear a student's radio show, where we discover the rare confluence of taste, his excitement at some song that he absolutely loves and cannot wait for us to hear, even as he does not expect this particular "us" to be listening. Or we happen across a campus demonstration, where our shy student is speaking passionately about a cause that matters to her for reasons we could not have anticipated. These are inspiring moments because we gain real insight into the mind that sits in our classroom, that submits work that is sometimes half-hearted, and that nonetheless tries to meet our expectations and pull a satisfactory grade.

And as teachers, we try to find ways to make these encounters with our whole students happen. It is one thing to come across the rare play, or radio show, or demonstration, but how can we gain that kind of insight into more than the occasional student mind? Sure, a few students might really shine during an in-class presentation, but the bulk respond to the assignment as just another paper. Others might thrive in a simulation of a real-life problem, where they whip out the toolkits they have filled in class and produce an ingenious solution, but meanwhile many of their classmates might not get into the exercise. A number of them will let their own whole-human-being voices speak in a letter written to a classmate, asking a real question instead of one designed to impress the teacher, but still others will not turn in the assignment or only ask the question they think they are supposed to ask. We constantly rack our brains, trying to come up with a variety of ways for students to respond so that each voice might speak at least once during the term. And with each new experiment, we discover a few voices we had never heard before, and we find new ways to respond to these newly-voiced concerns, ideas, ambitions.

The work in this collection represents the results of some recent brain-racking, where a group of teachers together tried some collaborative experiments. We recognized that what our assignments lacked was a chance for students to engage creatively with the material. After discussion together, we all went back to our classrooms and first asked our students to write poetry. We were all nervous about this, because we are not, after all, teachers of poetry. Furthermore, when we assigned poems, many of our students looked panicked. They had deliberately *not* signed up for creative writing. But then we were all thrilled—and our students were surprised—when we found that a lot of our students had found new ways into the material we were studying, just by writing poems about it. Sure, quite a few treated the assignment mechanically, maybe jotting down their poem over breakfast just to have something to turn in. But some were inspired to see the material from a point of view decidedly different from their own. Others had a great time playing with language to get across in layperson's terms how something technical works. Still others found a way to express their opinions without fear of teacher retribution. And a few gave a surprising and insightful reading of a difficult work, one that made us and the rest of the class *want* to re-examine the work, think about it some more.

Pleased with these results, many of us looked for other ways to allow students to respond creatively to material in the classroom. Teachers asked students to create graphic representations of course material, to design museum displays that presented a new way of looking at something familiar, to create futurist self-portraits that played with abstraction and technological methods to show something about the self. The more we played and invited our students to play, the more we were reminded of the real discoveries that can come from play.

Reflecting on this experimentation, we are very excited by what our students have done. We are inspired by how these assignments have shifted the usual dynamics of teaching and learning, allowing students to teach teachers as well as each other. We believe that others might similarly benefit from what we have learned, and we hope that what we have presented here might help other teachers to experiment in their own classrooms, to find new ways of hearing from their students.

Recent History of Teaching and Learning Creatively at Clemson

Growing out of Clemson University's nationally recognized Communication-Across-the-Curriculum (CAC) program, founded in 1990, the Poetry-Across-the-Curriculum (PAC) project began in 2000 as a search for new ways of using writing for learning, and specifically as a means of emphasizing creativity, new perspectives, and a wider range of ways for students to engage with course material. Over the next few years, more than forty teachers assigned students to write poetry about course subject matter and subsequently used those poems in creating an interactive community of learners in their classrooms. In 2004, some faculty suggested we encourage creative response in numerous ways to course topics, not just through poetry, and we began a Creative-Response-to-Learning (CRL) project. Students produced art work, music, altered books, collages, sculptures, videos, and multimedia presentations. Some CRL projects are represented in this collection. In 2005, the PAC and CRL projects merged into a single project, Teaching and Learning Creatively (TLC). More information about CAC and TLC at Clemson is available at http://www.clemson.edu/caah/Pearce/ and http://people.clemson.edu/~apyoung/projects/tlc.

As participants in the earlier PAC project, teachers from across campus assigned students to write a poem in response to material being taught. Usually these poems were considered informal responses, often ungraded, and thereby less wrought with pressure to meet a particular expectation. Students did not have to write great poems for the poems to succeed: teachers looked for evidence of engagement with course material, and also for creativity, playfulness with language, or a stimulating voice. They also found indications that students were bringing together material from across a course, or from more than one course, or combining lessons from the course with insights gathered elsewhere. Many students were able to see beyond the assignment, to become more invested in the ideas, issues, or substance of a particular course, forging connections between course material and a wider world. And many gained a higher degree of empathy for people affected by the issues or events taught in the course.

Many of us asked our students to write reflections to the poetry assignment. While some students got no more out of this assignment than any other assignment, others were surprised by the opportunity that the poetry assignment afforded, and were excited that they had done it, even though they might initially have resisted it. Others found that by assuming a voice other than their own they had room to try on ideas with which they were initially uncomfortable, or they had become more able to see a situation from a perspective very different from their own. And others felt that by being able to use humor or play, they could get more comfortable with the course material. The vast majority of student reflections agreed with the participating teachers: they were initially hesitant about the assignment, but really glad they had had the opportunity to confront course material in a new way. And many of them actually had fun doing it.

We were eager to "spread the word" to more teachers on campus. At the same time, we knew that while a few teachers might immediately think that asking students to write poetry in, say, a biology or psychology or zoology class was cool, many others would not be so sure. In the academy and outside, poetry is rarely thought to be as "useful" as other kinds of more information-oriented writing, and for some, it is—at best—a diversion from the real work and business of disciplinary knowledge. Furthermore, it is the rare teacher of chemistry who is comfortable enough with how poetry works to be willing to bring it into her classroom. And even in the world of CAC, poetry is not wholly welcome. While other forms of writing have been thought useful to the learning process—journals, letters, freewrites, e-mails—creative writing has rarely been introduced into the Across-the-Curriculum venture. Many teachers anticipate resistance from students asked to write poetry about topics that are not typically associated with poetry, particularly by those whose exposure to poetry has not been especially broad. (In a way, they are right: every semester, each time poetry is assigned, we encounter a fresh batch of resistance. And then, our students' collective surprise at what poetry allows.) In short, our question was, how do we convince teachers in a wide range of disciplines that it is not crazy to use poetry-writing as a tool of learning in the classroom?

As a part of our PAC project, we organized a number of different events to expose prospective participants to the benefits of the poetry assignment and encourage them to try it in their own classes. We held several workshops led by early, enthusiastic participants, who talked about how they used the assignment in their classes, what they had learned, and how students had reacted. These workshops gave a sense of the range of ways that teachers had employed the poetry assignment in their courses. A teacher of psychology had asked students to write a poem from the perspective of a person with a particular mental illness: she talked about how her students gained empathy for people affected by these disorders. A teacher of humanities had asked students to write a poem back to a modern artist: she told how the poetry writing made her students think harder about difficult paintings and find a voice for response. A teacher of biology assigned a whole series of poems over the course of the semester, and he explained how his students' reactions to the assignment changed over time and how their entire thought process was developed in part through work with the poems.

As a part of the workshops, we gave prospective participants tips for how to use the assignment in their classes. We encouraged them not to grade the assignment, but to keep it "low-stakes," so that students would be willing to take the risk of writing poems. We suggested that the poems be integrated into some classroom activity, so that students would have the chance to see each other's poems and learn from them. And we proposed that the teachers ask the students to write reflections on the process of writing poems for class: What had they learned? How did they write them? What was difficult? Exciting? Many of the teachers who participated in the workshops then went on to try the poetry assignment in their own classes.

As our community of participating teachers grew, we devised other activities to help the project succeed. We had a series of luncheon meetings, where teachers could talk with each other about what they were doing with the assignment, what worked well, what needed development. We gave poetry readings, often with the students themselves reading their poems. We made large posters of student poems, which were then posted around campus. Teachers participating in the project began to feel a sense of community with one another. Students found that they were asked to write poetry in a number of different classes. And poetry became a more normal part of the educational environment on campus.

While competition was not the ultimate goal of the project, teachers submitted exceptional examples of poems to a campus-wide "contest," whose winners received recognition on the PAC website and a gift certificate to the campus bookstore. Moreover, the judging sessions for these contests allowed teachers a chance to bring their work and experience together, and get new ideas from one another. From the discussions at the judging sessions, we compiled a deductive list of criteria: by seeing how judges made their choices, we could begin to determine what qualities they thought were necessary to a good student poem. We were surprised by how much agreement there was among judges about what made an effective poem. We pretty much agreed that a poem should express an idea not already said a million times, even as it expresses something that a wide variety of readers can identify with. We appreciated playfulness, detail, humor and cleverness, tension, ambition. We thought that the best poems had a sense of structure, or of narrative development, or a strong ending, or independence of the assignment. Developing this sense of what made successful poems made us better able to give our students direction in our assignments.

Inspired to experiment further with means of encouraging creativity in classes across the curriculum, many faculty began working on the Creative Response to Learning (CRL) project. This project had many of the same objectives as the PAC project, but it went beyond writing to other forms of creative expression—including portraits, sculptures, multi-media work, museum displays, and graphic syllabi. Teachers who encouraged students in a variety of creative media agreed with those who used poetry-writing that such projects enriched students' understanding of and investment in course material—and encouraged them to take a more active role in their education. Together, these projects have allowed students a wide range of ways to integrate creativity and fresh perspectives into their understanding and mastery of course content. And as we mentioned earlier, the PAC and CRL projects have merged to become one Teaching-and-Learning-Creatively project, thus inspiring the title of this book.

What's in this Book—and How to Use It

This collection presents a sampling of successful poems and creative responses produced as a part of these projects. Each student work is accompanied by a teacher's reflection, giving a flavor of the classroom situation for which the work was produced, and a sense of why the teacher found the work successful. As the years of work on these projects have progressed, more teachers have voiced a desire for the really good student work produced to reach a wider audience. From reading and seeing the works produced in our colleagues' classrooms, we have learned new ways of employing this assignment in our own. Colleagues who had not previously tried this kind of assignment in their own classrooms have found some of these works inspiring to their own teaching. This collection makes it easier to use students' creative responses to learning in classes.

These works represent a real dialogue between teachers and students. As creators of poems or illustrations, students are more willing to experiment with voice, and thereby find new words to express themselves. Graduate students who make graphic syllabi of courses they are about to teach, and undergraduates who create multi-media "concept maps" of courses they are taking, are better able to make sense of the "big picture" and understand how individual topics or units fit. In building designs for gardens, students take on a new medium, finding ways to propose solutions to global problems at the local level. And by imitating the methods used by experimental artists in order to create their own self-portraits, they gain a new understanding of the workings of materials and possibilities of experimental methods. Because these assignments step outside the parameters of regular graded work, students are often more willing to take risks with poems, to express unpopular ideas, or to ask probing questions that get to the heart of why material is being studied in the first place. And this shift in genre affects teachers' engagement with students as well. When a student creates something new in order to express ideas or ask questions, teachers are able to engage with the student in new ways—less judging, more willing to learn or rethink an idea, or experience a new way of seeing something.

A crucial part of the process is the teacher's response to the student's production, and we represent some of that response in the teachers' reflections that accompany each creative work. Even though these reflections are not addressed to the student, the fact that the students' work is being published means that the students and teachers are still in conversation. In essence, these reflections give something back to the student—a response to their work that goes beyond the usual grade and takes seriously the ideas they present and the language they use to present them. These reflections also show teachers learning from students, either about the material discussed, or about the student's outlook, or about themselves, or about what the student might see that the teacher did not.

These creative works and responses also give a sense of the kinds of communities that develop on campuses. Maureen McHugh, the author of "Fertilization Poem" and "Ode to Math (With Strategically Placed Vocabulary)," is not the only Clemson student to have written poems in more than one class and have those poems selected by judges for recognition. Sam Renken makes an appearance as the visiting cowboy poet in Skye Suttie's classroom, offering the challenge that leads to Kevin Howell's "My Post-Musheled Goolashuralphanoliacan Fluid Poem," and then a poem of Sam's appears in a stack of papers in Michael Neal's class, offering insight into a pedagogical problem. Jenn Miller first used poetry writing as a reflection vehicle in one course, but soon she was inspired to use it as a design tool in another. As a student, Emily Benthall Weathers writes "Looking into the Mirror" for Art Young's Victorian literature class, then becomes the teacher of her own class, reflecting on two students' poems that teach her about the texts she assigns. These are not coincidences: they are indications of the ways that "communication across the curriculum" refers not only to the need for writing and creativity in all classes, but also to the expanded forms of communication and new ways of making discoveries that grow from experimental, and even playful, pedagogy.

From these glimpses of other people's classrooms, we all return to our own classrooms, inspired to generate new dynamics and reflect on what new opportunities they might afford us.

The Editors
Clemson University
Spring 2006

Inspirations and Reflections

Clinical Psychology Practicum

How can I form a connection with a person who doesn't follow the norms for social interaction? Can I help someone change who is more likely to hit me or bite me than to smile and say, "Hello"?

Forming a therapeutic alliance with a client requires making an empathic connection. The symptoms of many psychiatric disorders interfere with the establishment of normal interpersonal relationships. Undergraduate students in their first clinical psychology practicum are often intimidated by the apparent strangeness of their clients' behaviors and distance themselves cognitively and emotionally, reducing the benefit of the interaction for both the client and the student. I have found that writing poems about the therapist-client interaction can provide a means for changing the student's perspective on the experience of mental illness.

Amanda Oberdoff's poem vividly describes her engagement in the life of an autistic boy. Through him she remembers details of her own childhood, parallels that connect the two of them despite the overt differences in their experiences. The poem captures the skilled clinical observer, who impassively records the child's behavior. Simultaneously, the emotional connection between therapist and child is activated, lending color and texture to the therapy session. Although she is the therapist and he is the client, Amanda lets us know that she isn't sure who benefits the most from the interaction.

Reading this poem helped me recapture the necessary humanness of the therapeutic relationship. Despite the artificial division between therapist and client, between therapy and friendship, all positive interactions have a symmetry and reciprocity. And all good clinical psychology students can find a connection that enables them to see past the sometimes unnerving client symptoms to the empathic understanding that binds us to our clients in the therapeutic relationship.

Jan Murdoch
Psychology

I watch those hands . . .

Amanda Oberdorff

I watch those hands that are still too small
To grasp what I carry with ease.
But while my own hands resign themselves
To the tasks that comprise adulthood
His move with frantic fascination
To interpret the details of life.
With black ink and pencil lead
I record the Crayola spectrum of his day.
And while he touches the worms and critters
Whose sensation I've long abandoned
I look at my own hands and wonder
Do my fingers point direction for him
Or is his easy grip pulling me
To the memories and excitement that age forgets?

Landscape Architecture Design

Jenn Miller was not required as part of her professional design studio to write "Fighting Sprawl: One Fence at a Time," although she had been required to write poems as reflection and documentation vehicles in two previous courses. For her project, Jenn proposed redesigning her grandmother's farm as an assisted living facility for aging farmers. Neighboring farmers no longer capable of cultivating the land are being shipped to sterile white rooms; the landscape surrounding the farms is threatened with dead-end cul-de-sac subdivisions. In an effort to preserve a way of life, Jenn strove to keep the aging population in an agricultural landscape.

How could Jenn, through her design, halt the encroaching bulldozer and characterless suburban sprawl? Frustrated with her initial results and passionate about saving the farm, Jenn decided to continue developing the project in a directed studies class. It was during this re-envisioning and redevelopment of the project that she turned to writing a poem. Poetry was now a design tool rather than a reflection and documentation vehicle as in previous classes.

From drawing, Jenn switched to creating a verbal and visual poem. Composing this poem jogged her loose from her stuck position, and launched her forward beyond a nostalgia for times past; through the poem she roots herself firmly in the present while protecting the future. Her professional training teaches her to gather information, analyze, synthesize, arrive at a concept, develop the design, present a proposal—a solution. Writing the poem accomplished what other vehicles of a design process could not: in a few words she summarizes a past, critiques the present, and stubbornly confronts the encroaching future.

Reinforcing the firmness and stubbornness of farmers and fences, the graphic layout of the poem describes thin, barbed wire at angles—far from the picturesque notion of quaint split rail or white picket fences. There is an honesty portrayed in the visual poem: lines askew, reacting to invisible forces.

More so than the array of some 30 professional drawings and documents to describe her project intentions, a mere 8 lines powerfully sum them up. Just as in Pablo Neruda's poem "Poetry," "And it was at that age . . . Poetry arrived in search of me"; so it was with Jenn—when passion for her grandmother's farm stifled and frustrated her, from some dark alleyway of the mind, Poetry called her name.

Frances F. Chamberlain
Landscape Architecture

Fences

Jenn Miller

FIGHTING SPRAWL: ONE FARM AT A TIME

MY FENCES ARE MADE OF WIRE AND WOOD
POST AND LINE THEY STAND TO FRAME
BUILT TO KEEP IN CATTLE AND LIKE
BUT NOW STAND ONLY TO HOLD FEARS OUT
LIVES HAVE COME AND FENCES FORGOTTEN
AS MY EYESIGHT FAILS SO DO MY FENCES
FIGHTING FOR FENCES HAS WEATHERED ME
BUT MY FENCES WILL NOT FALL

Victorian Literature

"Looking into the Mirror" invites a fresh perspective on prejudice, dangerous stereotypes, and anti-Semitism. In a Victorian literature class, I often ask students to write a dramatic monologue, a poetic form made famous by Robert Browning and Alfred Tennyson. The speaker in a dramatic monologue is not the writer but a character the writer has imaginatively created. In this poem, Rebecca Rosenberg is quite distinct from the author, Emily Benthall Weathers. Rebecca is a Jew; Emily is not.

From the first line, I see through the eyes of Rebecca, looking in a mirror at the bags under her eyes and her altered nose. In the four stanzas, I move with Rebecca from humorous banter at work about Italian ethnicity, to privileges of southern Protestantism, to an ignorant, cruel, and unexpected verbal attack, to voicing repressed anger as the innocence of a Jewish childhood confronts inexplicable prejudice.

The prejudice is pervasive. Rebecca moves from a Mississippi culture that excludes Jews from organizations like sororities and where it is best to not acknowledge a Jewish heritage to what she expects to be a "so different" New York City, where ethnicity is acknowledged and often celebrated, whether on *Sopranos* or *Seinfeld.* But New York City, in the person of Brad, so hot with his arm around Rebecca's waist, is not so different after all. I feel my own anger rising at Brad's arrogant, dangerous, and cruel demeaning of people based on a name, a religion, or a slightly altered nose.

The last two stanzas end with questions, images that express the paradoxical feelings of a young woman wanting to fit in and yet wanting to maintain her identity. The final question is asked of all of us. We are all part of the human family, and Christians and Jews share similarities in religious heritage, so why so much hatred and prejudice?

I asked Emily about this poem that moves me so deeply. She told me she has a favorite cousin, a Jew who tells wonderful, humorous stories about the foolish and ignorant anti-Semitic experiences she encounters. In her poem, Emily retells these stories with a rising anger that her cousin does not display. Emily imagines her cousin's experiences as her own, and in doing so, she provides me with fresh and compelling images of my world.

Art Young
Victorian Literature

16

Looking into the Mirror

Emily Benthall Weathers

How did these bags appear, underneath my eyes, brown,
Brown eyes; rich, brown hair—*crown of a woman's glory*—
But the imperfect nose has been altered—a bit more streamlined.
Circles, not enough sleep. Busy day at work when
    "REBECCA!" yelled from across the floor to my counter
    "What are you doing for Christmas? I bet
"Your family eats the Turkey, stuffing, and all
    " . . . don't they?"
"Yeah. What are you doing, eating pasta?"
    "Everyone thinks that because I'm Italian
    "All we do is sit around, talk, and eat pasta."
—Came the thick accented response, arms flailing—
    " . . . we do."
    "And everyone thinks that afterwards we watch the *Sopranos*
    "Well . . . we do."

Sopranos, Seinfeld, working at Saks Fifth Avenue,
New York, so different from the South.
Couldn't wait to get to New York
Leaving—University of Mississippi—such a southern school.
And how *did* I get into Chi O?
Mom's Methodist (or used to be before she married dad)
And Mrs. Jenny—Presbyterian—put in a good word for me
(not one word about dad).

Brad . . . that night—and was he hot!—
Flirting over a beer, similar interests:
'80's music, theater, travel—and he had talent:
"How long have you played the guitar? Can you play . . ."
The most fun I've had—
Until the anti-Semitic jokes surfaced
Brutal—shock . . . resume air of confidence, Rebecca.
Hello! I'm standing right here.
Yet his ignorance continued:
" . . . would never date one of them . . . and you know their noses"
Hello! You! you with your arm around my waist,
Did I mention my last name?
Rosenberg. R –O –S –E –N –B –E –R –G
Like the nose job?

Growing up thought it meant having a bat mitzvah,
Being guaranteed eight gifts come winter,
Eating matzo balls, sitting shiva,
Hear, O Israel: The Lord our God, the Lord is one!
    "The Jews, the Jews killed Jesus!" Jesus Christ our Savior.
Christ!
But, this same Jesus, Jewish,
"King of the Jews,"
Right?

General Biology

The poet William Butler Yeats once said, "Education is not the filling of a pail, but the lighting of a fire." Physical flames need three things to sustain them: fuel, oxygen, and heat. I believe there are three analogous components of the educational "fire triangle": course content, student/teacher interaction, and a spark of creativity. When I teach biology, there is never any shortage of the first two components of this triangle. The challenge is to find the creativity that sparks novel thinking in my students. I have discovered that having them write creative poetry serves as a kind of mental kindling that fuels new understanding.

An excellent example is Maureen McHugh's "Fertilization Poem," written in an honors section of Introductory Biology at Clemson University. Maureen chose "poetic art" to contrast the reproductive investments of males and females. Evolutionary theory argues that, because of their abundant and easily manufactured sperm, males are rather cavalier about (and eager for) mating opportunities. Females, on the other hand, need to protect their valuable eggs and thus should be choosy when selecting mates. Maureen takes this evolutionary battle of the sexes and translates it into a witty repartee between the stereotyped pickup lines of men and the more discerning response of a woman. She humorously but accurately depicts the fundamental biology by casting the men's abrupt lines as competitive sperm swimming about the egg, comparing these with the lengthy and thoughtful response of the woman shown in the coiled text of her egg. The visual layout not only is accurate in its anatomical depiction, but also forces the reader to physically engage in the poem by rotating the page in order to read what is being said. I find Maureen's design as absorbing and fundamentally important to the learning being demonstrated as is the process of fertilization to life itself.

Maureen's poem is exemplary, but I have many other student poems that demonstrate equally creative processing of course content to yield deeper understanding. I am left feeling that Yeats was right, and that with poetry we have yet another way to light the fire of education.

Jerry A. Waldvogel
Biological Sciences

Fertilization

Maureen McHugh

Go ahead and break through my glorious vile; the acids did many of your friends corrode. But you have made it through a dangerous road; you have already been through the difficult trials, and you've reached me whom you so desire. You want to combine your DNA with mine? Haploid or diploid or so you pine. Well, go ahead and pine after me. We'll see which one's the most lucky. We've only this chance to fulfill our fate. Many have tried and many will fail.

coffee because I grind fine

'Cause you've been running through my mind all day. Well, do you have that effect on me?

I've lost my phone number can I have yours? I know

let's get it on... so nice so warm...

Do you know karate? 'Cause your body is really kicking.

Are you from Tennessee? 'Cause you're the only 10 I see.

21

Abnormal Psychology

When I was 5 years old, I walked into school for the first time and I never left. At its best, a classroom is a magical place: a community of minds and senses, each contributing pieces of the puzzle in a collaborative quest for understanding.

That's where poetry comes in.

In my Abnormal Psychology class, I assign poetry writing to encourage *informed empathy,* knowledge about mental illness and its treatment combined with an understanding of its personal impact on individuals, families, and caregivers. When I first assigned poetry, my intention was to enhance *students'* learning: to give them a voice, to surprise themselves and their classmates with fresh ways of seeing. To my great joy, I've discovered that their poems do the same for me.

In just 21 lines, Laurie Gambrell creates a highly evocative portrait of "The Mental Health Professional." The therapist's exhaustion, ambivalence, and persistence come through in Laurie's repetition of "oozing" and her decision to capitalize only one word in the entire poem: "She."

Laurie's words and rhythms invite me to reflect on my own experience as a clinical psychologist. I scribble notes, images her poem evokes for me: memories of working with a young woman diagnosed with "borderline personality disorder," whose profound sense of abandonment and bottomless feelings of anger and emptiness erupted in years of suicidal thoughts and self-destructive behaviors. Laurie's poem echoes my struggle to maintain healthy boundaries while working with someone who needed so much; the simultaneous privilege and burden of bearing witness to her deliberations of whether to live or die, and the unspoken questions: Am I giving therapeutic support? Or fostering dependency? Do I care enough? Or too much? Am I helping? Or hurting? And without intending to do so, my brainstorming-on-paper takes the shape of a poem:

> Boundaries.
> Borderline.
> Burnout.
> all Bs—or not to bes
> what is the question?

A poet gets the ball rolling: provoking, surprising, questioning . . . and inviting the reader to add her own spin. Thank you, Laurie, for bringing your magic into our classroom.

Patricia A. Connor-Greene
Psychology

The Mental Health Professional

Laurie Gambrell

have you ever made cornbread
watched the golden batter hit the hot
skillet and ooze
bubbling and slow to fill the pan

have you ever been frustrated
felt it slide over your hot
skin and ooze
bubbling and slow to fill the core
of you

i feel the oozing (is that even a real word?)
it doesn't matter if it is or isn't or wasn't or couldn't be

because all i feel is the ooze
the utter ooziness of the ooze is oozing

because i know that
it doesn't matter if it is tricyclic antidepressants or lithium or
benzodiazepines or chickennoodlesoup

because i know that
it doesn't matter if it is four days or two weeks or thirteen years

because i know that She will be back
in my office oozing her life

into my pan of golden cornbread

Women's Body Image in Popular Culture

In my course students investigate the images of women's bodies in such media as television, magazines, and movies. A sexualized body image is becoming significantly more prevalent, with sometimes devastating results.

For young girls, a desire to imitate models and rock stars can lead to dress and demeanor that broadcast mixed signals. Hayley Shilling's outstanding poem, "Going Downtown," dissects this ambivalence for college students. With almost every word and phrase, she punctuates the problematic behavior of young women dressing up to go downtown and participate in a college ritual of meeting guys in bars.

In the first stanza, she subtly reveals the young women's strategy in wearing "few layers" in February with "strappy shoes." With the comfort of numbers ("our twenty toes"), they present themselves to the men inside. She suggests their vulnerability when they look for someone, "drunk enough to say hello (to the likes of us) we think."

She shows the caution they use, drinking slowly, even if they swirl the "ice looking for warmth." They are imminently conscious of the competition and are alternately "jealous and sorry for them," those girls with "longer hair, shorter skirts, higher boots." But the undercurrent of possible dangerous sex jars the reader:

Old men say, "you look like my daughter, want to dance?"

Young men say, "I'll be your daddy, what's in your glass?"

They know that what they are wearing has an impact, but they are "just girls, going downtown."

Hayley has captured extremely well the pitfalls of our highly sexual culture. Her incisive poem communicates a sense of anticipation and excitement but doesn't come without some nod to the problems "girls just having fun" can face— "hunting and hunted, going downtown." Hayley's choice of words, phrasing, and the ambivalence she instills in the poem reflect the sometimes casual choices young women make that can become so destructive. They are just girls going downtown, but in reality they are young women flirting with possible devastation.

Judith M. Melton
Women's Studies

Going Downtown

Hayley Shilling

We wear few layers
And go out into rainy February looking for warmth.
Our twenty white toes, pinched by high shoes, strappy shoes, click on the
    side walk and
Pinken from cold air, and the friction of
Going downtown.
We open doors, present ourselves to bouncers—bona fide by age.
We present ourselves to men inside
All the time casting our eyes around for a tall body, a shock of dark hair,
Someone
Not too drunk to speak, but drunk enough to say hello
(to the likes of us) we think.
Often the place is only partially filled and we move on.
Two approach, stools change, bouncers change
(They know our faces, if not our names)
And again we slip out into the rain
Hunting and hunted, going downtown.

We order a few drinks
And down them slowly, swirling the ice looking for warmth.
Our beautiful painted lips, pursed around short straws, bitter
disguised liquid,
Pinken from Sex on the Beach and
Going downtown.

Sometimes the loud music makes it all worth it if it's something we recognize,
And there's someone there too,
From classes or from last Friday to pretend to be interested in shouting at our ears and hearing us over it,
Or notice we made ourselves up to show them.
Other girls have longer hair, shorter skirts, higher boots, and we're jealous and sorry for them.
Old men say, "You look like my daughter, want to dance?"
Young men say, "I'll be your daddy, what's in your glass?"
They compliment our clothes and grab our ass
We're just girls, going downtown.

Modern Rhetoric

The world I inhabit is primarily a mediated one. Most of what I *know,* I know because I read about it, see it, or hear it via a media conduit which, more often than not, relies upon words to make meaning. I'm comfortable with the mediation, at least partially because it allows me to know about many things—some of them scary, dangerous, even tragic—at a safe distance. The flip side of this, however, is what those of us who revel in the power of language understand—that *sometimes* words allow us to see, touch, taste, smell, *feel* things in a way that transcends mere understanding. This is a journey that begins and ends on a page, but takes the reader far away in the interim.

In "The Past is History" Maura Shaughnessy traces that journey, both with words and with the visuals she uses to enhance her poem. She starts as readers start, with a book, page numbers, and words. But quickly, the realities of the subject matter eclipse the words, and as she illustrates with the bronze plaques in the title and the footsteps that march across the page, it becomes clear that the story neither begins nor ends with what is written there. A critical, if sometimes traumatic part of education is learning that there is always "more than words," on pages 33–45.

We word-lovers know that words have real effects. When we share the poem, the picture, the essay or news story that hits students right in the gut or that leaves them unable to sleep, we're encouraging them to join us in going beyond the finite information to which we have direct access and instead, open themselves to experiences that are only accessible to us through the words or pictures of others. Maura reminds us that reading is only a small part of this process. For it to "work" the reader must open herself to the text, considering not just what is on the page, but what is behind it. Clearly, this is not without risk. The payoff, however, is that when you open yourself to the words, they become part of who you are; the experiences become, to some extent, your own, and when that happens, you trade the safety of distance for the wisdom that comes with knowing, understanding, *feeling* things from another point of view. *That* is the process of education.

Teddi Fishman
English

The Past Is History

Maura Shaughnessy

The **PAST** is **HISTORY**

By Maura Shaughnessy

Students
Turn to page 33 of your history books
Remove your fingers from your ears
Listen closely, and you might hear
Shreds of sentences, echoes of final laments,
shadows of sighs.
Don't be discouraged if you find only silence-
Despair was often mute.
Pale faces mirroring pale skies,
White threads of spider web clouds
That slinked into thunderous swastikas
without warning,
Bathing our brothers and sisters in toxic messages:
"Violence is generous"
"Violence is therapy"
"Violence is healing,
Restoring,
Cleansing."
But children aren't rosy and shining
They are bloody rags, dull and lifeless
Our mothers and fathers are starved
Of sleep, food, life.
I see you
squirming in your seats.
Resist the urge to blind your eyes
Read between the lines. There is so much
More than words, on pages
33-45.

Landscape Design

When I ask my landscape design students to write about their favorite childhood space, I am always struck by how many of those spaces are defined by water, and how, like Ishmael, we all want to get "as nigh to the water as we possibly can without falling in." Renee Keydoszius' design of a children's water garden for the South Carolina Botanical Garden evokes memories of my own childhood spent wading through fern glades bordering the streams and pools leading down to the lake of my youth. Her imaginative design provides opportunities for children to seek and experience water, the most desired and least provided element in a child's play world.

Exploring the beautifully rendered paths of her design allows one to circumambulate the spiraling trail to the fiddlehead courtyard. I imagine children in the "Sprouting Wings" after-school nature-based program discovering tadpoles swimming in Renee's "Leaping Frog Pond." I'm moved by the designer's ability to weave art, science, and environmental education opportunities into this project focusing on the role of water in the environment. As children explore and play "hide and seek" beneath the willow branches, they can observe how plants, animals, and humans depend on and enjoy water. Aquatic plants are grouped in zones determined by water depth, and submerged plants grow beneath the water's surface, taking up carbon dioxide and releasing oxygen for fish and other wildlife. Spawning areas and protective hiding places for young fish are provided with submerged, floating, and marginal aquatic plants.

Renee and her fellow students were certified by the National Wildlife Federation as "Habitat Stewards" for their service learning work on the Children's Garden project at the South Carolina Botanical Garden. I applaud their ability to use critical thinking and creative design to address global issues at the local level while networking with community and national partners to create stimulating spaces for wildlife and children to share. Renee's work instills in me a renewed desire to splash, spray, conserve, and celebrate *water* and the multitude of life that it sustains.

Mary Taylor Haque
Landscape Architecture

Children's Water Garden

Renee Keydoszius

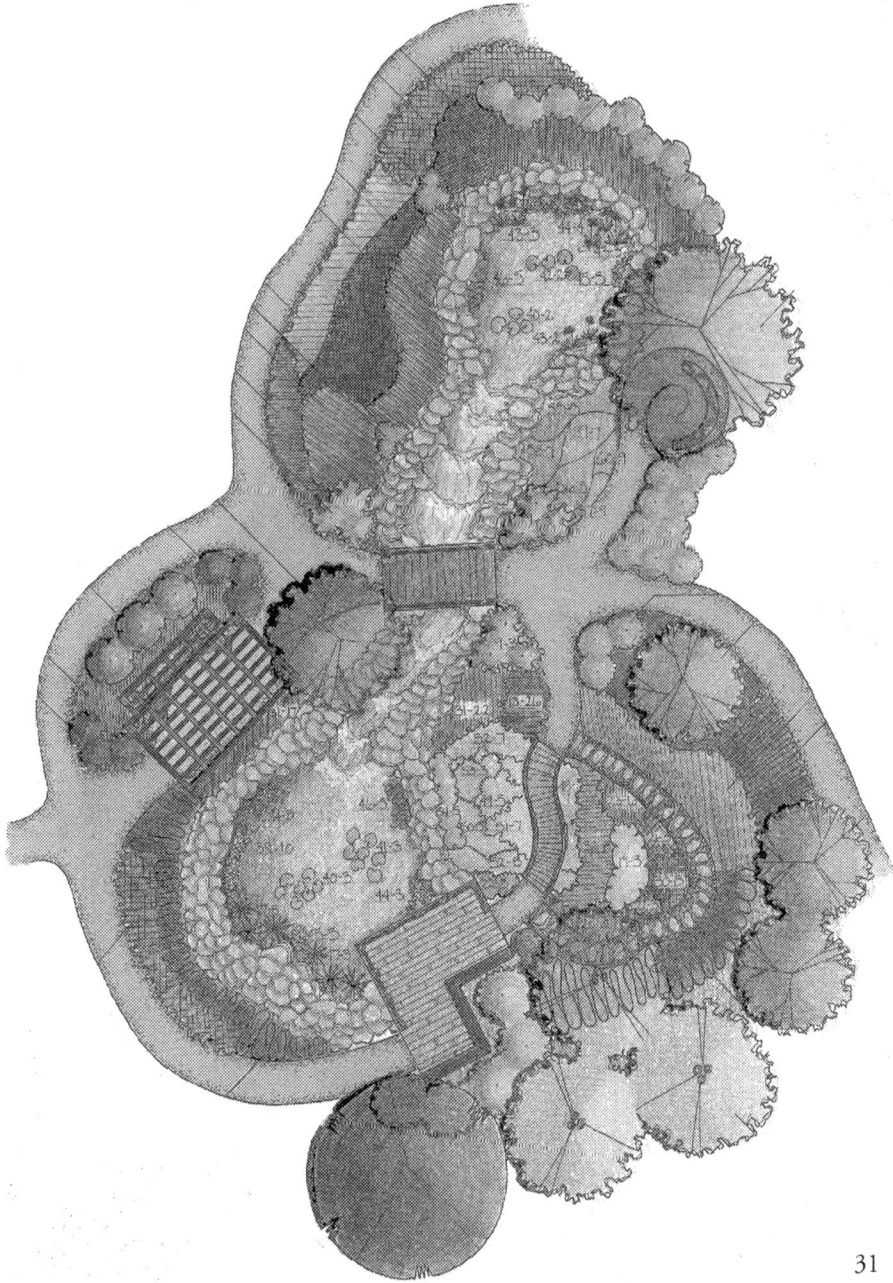

Sociology Field Placement

A principal goal of sociology is to teach students how social structure impacts their personal lives. To help students make this connection I provide them with opportunities to "take the role of the other" and view the world through someone else's eyes. Developing such understanding facilitates the development of trust, empathy and compassion.

Poetry has allowed my students to explore these themes of social structure and taking the role of others. I often ask my Field Placement students to write a poem from the perspective of an agency client. I encourage them to consider several questions: What is your client's life like? How are his or her life experiences different from yours? How does it feel to be a client of your agency?

Students have submitted poems about a variety of clients, including a domestic violence victim, a man "freed" from jail but placed on parole, a truant teenager, and a homeless veteran. The poem "Just a Child" was written by Michelle Love, a student who interned at the Department of Social Services. She wrote the poem from the perspective of a child caught up in the foster care system. After reading her poem to the class, Michelle described the emotional connection she had with her clients and how such connections were shaped by her role as a mother. She realized her own children were like her clients, except for one major factor: her clients did not have the warmth, stability, and security associated with most parent-child relationships.

This assignment has changed how I think about my students. I began to question how empathic I was toward my students and whether such an understanding shaped my relationships with them. I was reminded that each of my students was once "just a child," with fears and vulnerabilities similar to those described in Michelle's poem. In the past several years, students have told me stories about being homeless, living in foster care, being a victim of domestic violence, or escaping poverty. In the end, Michelle's poem reminds me to walk in the shoes of my students to better understand how broader social forces and personal experiences may shape their learning and understanding of the course material.

Catherine Mobley
Sociology

Just a Child

Michelle Love

You may see me as just a child
I know I am only five,
But I have grown up very fast
Just trying to stay alive.

I love my mommy and daddy
I don't know where they have gone,
I miss them very much
And I don't want to be alone.

My foster parents are nice
And my new room is great,
I love my new school
It's the system I hate.

I have to see my caseworker
Every other week,
I see my parents once a month
And they kiss me on the cheek.

They say they didn't mean
To hurt me or make me cry,
My caseworker says if I go home
There's a possibility I could die.

I wish we could be a family
Like we were before,
One without the drugs and drinking
And with love once more.

I don't want DSS to have
Custody of me,
I want to be a little boy
I just want to be free.

I want to laugh and play and
Not be concerned with seeing the judge,
I don't want to be in DSS custody
I am beginning to hold a grudge.

I just want to be normal
And do what little boys do,
I don't want to be hit or
Punched or kicked with a shoe.

You may see me as just a child
I know I am only five,
But I have grown up very fast
Just trying to stay alive.

Natural Resource Economics

Economists typically use graphs, tables, or charts to communicate, but rarely use pictures. So one day, instead of asking my Resource Economics students to draw supply and demand graphs to illustrate the changes that had occurred in Western timber markets over the past three decades, I told them to draw two pictures, one reflecting the situation in the 1980s and one the situation today. This was one of many group assignments, with the students working in the same group all semester.

The 1980s were a transitional period in timber markets, from one of active harvest and thriving mills to one of regulatory delays, environmental battles, and reductions in timber harvest. While most groups showed healthy forests and harvesting in the first picture and conflict, lack of harvesting, and unhealthy forests in the second picture, the group whose work is shown here (Ralph Burrell, Brandon Durant, Amelia French, Beth Jordan, and Keelie Shealy) more accurately illustrated healthy forests with some harvesting activity, but also conflict and regulation ("No Cut Zone") and the resulting decrease in mill activity and trucking loads all in the first picture. Their second picture shows the consequences of these changes on forest health (infested and dying trees), mills (most are gone), lumberjacks (none shown), and trucking (long drives).

This assignment allowed the students to "see" the interrelationships among the forests, lumberjacks, mills, and trucking, as well as the impact of activities in one time period on each market later in time. They also had fun and are probably more likely to remember the lessons of this assignment than if I had asked them to graph the changes. While it is important for students of economics to be able to communicate using graphical analysis, alternative representations of economic relationships such as this can help them learn as well, if not better, while also improving their ability to communicate economic concepts to others.

Molly Espey
Applied Economics and Statistics

1980s' Western Timber Markets

Ralph Burrell, Brandon Durant, Amelia French, Beth Jordan, Keelie Shealy

Today's Western Timber Markets

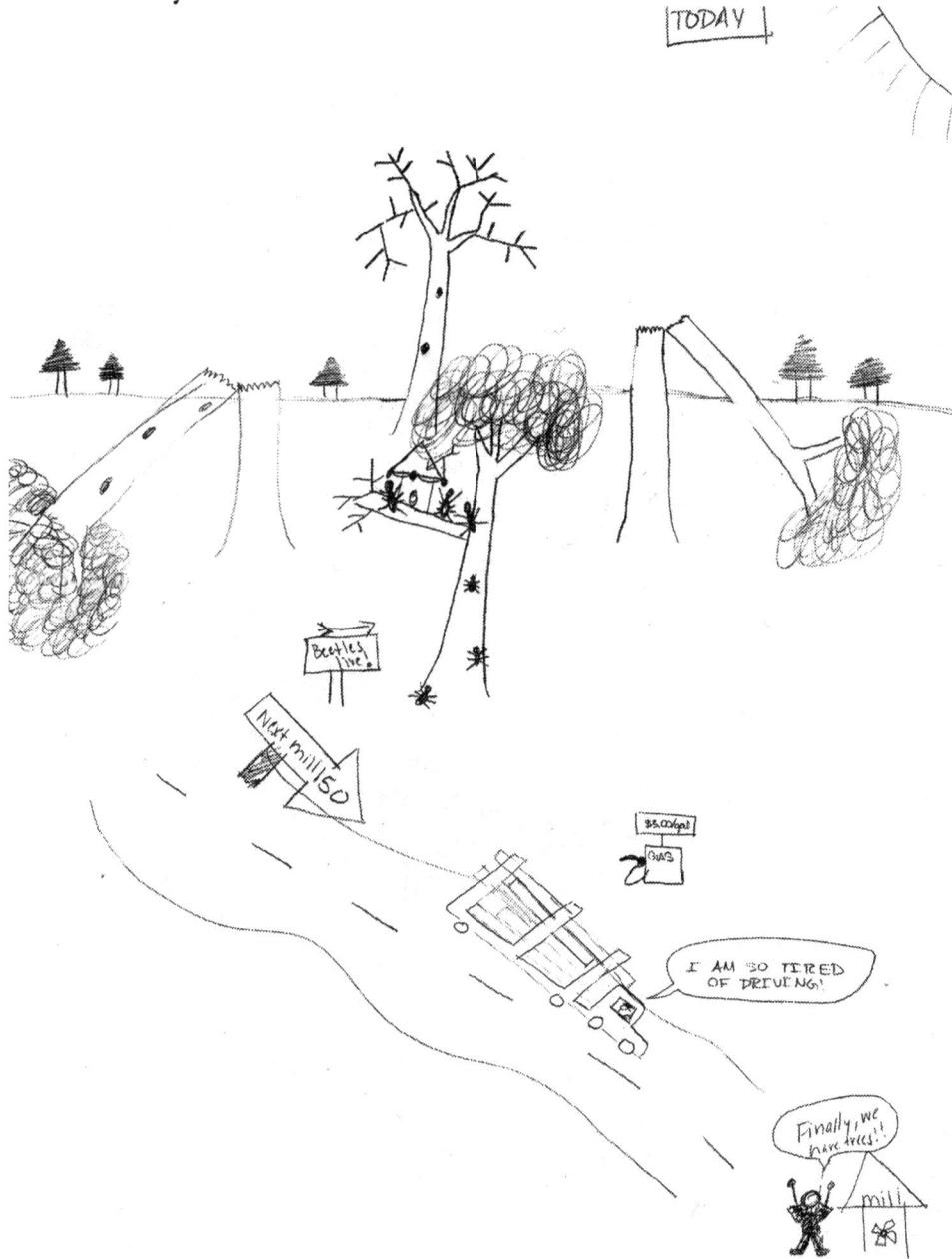

Museums and Modern Culture

Writing a poem can offer a student, silenced by school, a chance to enter a larger conversation.

In my interdisciplinary general-education humanities course about museum culture, students examine how museums present objects, represent cultures, and acculturate visitors into accepting their understanding. We also look at art that responds to museums—including poems.

One of the first hurdles in the course, though, is students' fear of museums. They worry that everyone else "gets it," while they remain in the dark. This fear is especially prominent in our discussions of modern art.

During this discussion, students write poems engaging an artwork in conversation. By this time we have talked about how works of art respond to museums and can challenge the museum's ability to determine how people are supposed to see. Their poems, I point out, are a chance for them to talk back to the art and the museums.

Jason Snelgrove's poem about Marcel Duchamp's *Nude Descending a Staircase* (1912) playfully interprets the painting, while changing the feel of the work. The painting depicts a nude woman coming down the stairs by breaking her body into a bunch of small planes: she has become a collection of surfaces over time, reproducing the movement of her descent. It is a hard painting, by which I mean a painting of hard surfaces—not the softness one might associate with bodies. In a sense, the painting demolishes the body to represent motion.

But Jason's poem gives the nude's body back its softness, its humanity: there is a person composed of all those surfaces. She is actively rushing, maybe talking, but no, not talking after all. The speaker wants to understand what she is thinking and to explain her appearance through her intentions. The woman is conscious that she is presenting herself, even though she has rejected the expected. The gentle humor in the last line—that the entire show is about shaved legs—adds another kind of humanity, one that is self-aware but not self-conscious. Returning to Duchamp's painting, a reader of Jason's poem finds the "masterpiece" is transformed by the student's creation.

Catherine E. Paul
English

Nude Descending a Staircase

Jason Snelgrove

Watch her rush down the staircase.
No, she pauses. She stops, she isn't walking.
Is she talking?
No, she can't—she has no time.
She must continue her descent.
So much ado over today!
Everyone is awaiting her presence.
The debutante enters her ball.
Startling, she's naked.
Did all the preparation pass in vain?
No, for I see she is aware of her new state.
She appears to have recently shaved her legs.

Community Health

Darci Rubin's poem, "Care Begins With Understanding," began as an assignment for my nursing course. During this semester my clinical group of nursing students worked with a local pastor to plan and conduct a health fair for the local Hispanic population. Since my students are generally non-Spanish speakers, I encourage them to step outside their comfort zones and learn Spanish phrases to facilitate communication with their clients. Each semester I tell my students how important it is to recognize cultural influences that impact health care. I share experiences of living in a Latin American country and how frightening or frustrating it can be when you don't understand the language being spoken. My goal for students is to recognize that communication is a basic requirement as we strive to meet the cultural needs of clients.

Darci has taken this concept of cultural competence that I present in the classroom and transformed it into real-life application. She thinks about the impact of lack of communication and understands the legal implications of making sure her client is able to make an informed consent for medical procedures. While we worked with Hispanic clients this semester, her translation of the phrase "care begins with understanding" into various languages indicates that she recognizes the need for all ethnic groups to be understood in their own language.

As I read her poem I can feel the frustration she experiences as she faces an ethical dilemma. Can she truly give quality care when this void exists as she tries to communicate? Darci's creative poem sets the stage for the reader to experience the nurse's role in a difficult situation. The thoughts and feelings that are expressed in the poem reflect Darci's empathy, but she takes it a step further by encouraging nurses and the community to take action, promoting improved care through understanding and communication.

A teacher can present a model or concept in the classroom, but when the student puts it into action in a real-world situation then learning has truly taken place. Darci's poem plays with language and demonstrates that for the nurse, as for the writer, care begins with understanding.

Roxanne Amerson
Nursing

Care Begins with Understanding

Darci M. Rubin

Care begins with understanding.
As I walk into your home, I only know your name.
The spelling and the sound of it just isn't quite the same.
To offer unconditional care
Is the reason that I'm there.

El cuidado empieza con la comprension.
My practice is holistic for everyone I meet.
I strive to serve the differing needs of strangers on the street.
Designing a unique plan of care is paramount to assure,
that your needs are met in such a way that lend themselves to cure.

Le soin commence avec la comprehension.
Anyone can take your arm and wrap it in a cuff.
To hand you a pill or paper script and assume you understand would be a bluff.
To offer you the best level of care seems difficult to obtain.
How does a nurse struggle with this conflict, this constant strain?

La cura inizia con capire.
How will I know you understand the demands of this illness?
As we sit together amongst this language barrier of stillness.
How can I ascertain you know the intricacies of its care?
These are the common frustrations we both must share.

Sorge beginnt mit Verstandnis.
I have to utilize your family members to offer up my care.
How can I know what is said and understood when I am unaware?
They never advised linguistics while we were in school.
I guess they thought that our words, our ways, would always be the rule.

De zorg begint met begrip.
The cross section of cultures in our communities continue to quickly change,
And yet the ways of learning haven't been rearranged.
How can I grant my signature to document informed consent of care?
I cannot assume you understand, and risk that I may err.

O cuidado comecacom entendimento.
We all must come together, nurses and the community, to advocate a change.
Learn all about each other, the words, the sounds, and the range.
It is only through understanding and comprehension that we can combat the fear.
We need to offer culturally competent care and fulfill the mission of nursing, our career.

Care begins with understanding.

Landscape Architecture Design

Less is more.

This provocative architectural maxim is intriguing to design students who begin to explore its meaning, often for the first time, in their early design studio experiences.

Our Landscape Architecture undergraduates come from a world of pre-packaged vignettes, where ideas are pre-digested for them by Google™, where reading between the lines is unnecessary. Just the facts, please . . . Give me the key words.

For many, design is about more for less—more product for less cost, more answers in less time, more academic bang for the buck. So in our introductory design studio class, where we learn to generate and evaluate ideas, we encourage students to take the time to think things through. Even when the result is a one-page drawing, we like to see a dozen background sketches and diagrams en-route.

The trick is to be selective—to work at developing the best design solution and resist accepting the first one. The language of design stresses this important distinction between basic simplification and careful reduction to essence.

Poetry employs our most familiar language to exemplify this concept. Poetry is about attentive selection—about larger ideas portrayed by a few quality words and phrases. Elegant design addresses several problems with a singular solution. This haiku-style poem, by second-year Landscape Architecture student Elisabeth Simmons, reads:

> As a traveller
> I walk the ant lines alone—
> We think together

To better understand the nature of "landform" Elisabeth created a number of corrugated terrain compositions in a sandbox, crossing an initial grid-like format with contrasting earth-marks and parallel pathways. These were inspired by close-up studies (charcoal drawings) of her own palm, with its contoured skin-ridges and dynamic crevices.

In placing herself into this intimate topography she imagined herself responding to the "sandscapes" she had created by shrinking herself down to the scale of living inhabitant.

As such, she journeyed into and around this composition.

In presenting this mindset to us Elisabeth acknowledges the collaborative nature of sharing the design experience—of communicating basic concepts—by bringing us into her space. Through this haiku we readers can become, in effect, prospective clients.

David Chamberlain
Landscape Architecture

As a Traveller

Elisabeth Simmons

As a traveller,
I walk the ant lines alone.
We think together.

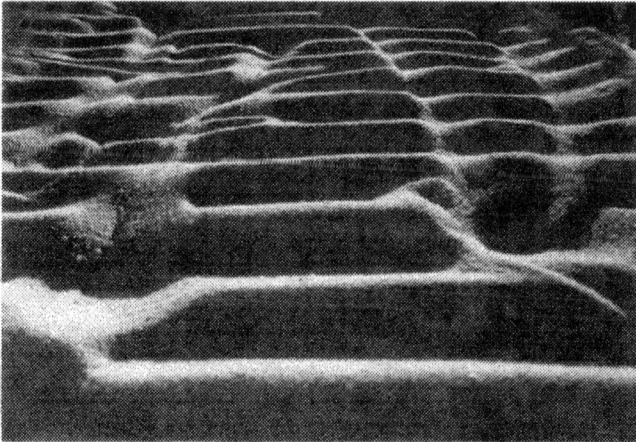

Professional Practice in Industrial Engineering

I coordinate a seminar series for our junior-level industrial engineering students. Michelle Hatcher wrote this poem in response to a guest speaker's presentation on "Diversity in the Workplace." I liked it especially for its attitude. The voice in the poem isn't one of bitterness, but rather one of concern, for what we all lose when prejudice enters the workplace. And that's just the point I was hoping my students might consider, given the focus of the seminar series.

As Michelle points out, we differ from each other in highly visible ways (affluence, race, gender) and these differences tend to evoke prejudices. But there are many dimensions on which we may be similar to or different from others, only a few of which are apparent at first encounter. Isn't it likely we have much in common with many of the people we meet who are most visibly different from us, perhaps more than we have with the people we interact with each day who look just like us?

I enjoyed the picture the speaker paints of herself being let "out of the box." In engineering, we talk a lot about generating creative solutions to intractable problems by thinking "outside the box." I think what Michelle is getting at here is that diversity in the workplace supports thinking outside the box. As the speaker says, she is "a person who has a lot to offer that you'll never experience." In today's global marketplace, organizations must offer products and services that meet people's needs while taking into account differences in age, gender, language, culture, size, shape, and infirmity. Diversity is something that people within organizations must learn to use to competitive advantage, not something that people must simply learn to manage. As Michelle's poem indicates, diversity in the workplace brings a diversity of experiences into the development process that enable the creation of new products and services that better meet people's needs.

Joel Greenstein
Industrial Engineering

Diversity

Michelle Hatcher

Rich, poor, black, white, male, female,
no matter who you are, no one is the same.

Church, school, home, job,
no matter where you go there is diversity.

It doesn't matter who you are or where you are, diversity plays a part in
    the game.
Why can't you accept me? I know I'm not the same.
You already have me labeled and don't even know my name.

I know I don't look or act like you, but should I be treated differently?
Actually, I'm glad I'm not like you, it just wasn't meant to be.

I don't get invited out for lunch or asked to the company picnic.
I am a person who has a lot to offer that you'll never experience.
Let me out of the box and then you'll stop being so tense.
Talk to me, connect with me, let go of that mental baggage.
Then we can laugh and interact without a person's feelings being
    damaged.

No matter who you are, no one is the same.
No matter where you go, there is diversity.

Composition Theory

From the moment I read Sam Renken's poem "Cat," the morbid central image—that of the author using a piece of steel railway footing to put a dying cat out of its misery—was etched into my mind where I assume it will remain for many years. When I first heard about this collection, I didn't want to write about Sam's poem because he is an English graduate student who specializes in creative writing. It seemed akin to cheating for me to include his poem because a central principle for Poetry Across the Curriculum is showcasing student poetry from disciplines other than English, where one might typically expect to read and write poetry. Yet Sam's poem provides me with a different understanding of the subject and students I teach, one upon which I have found value reflecting.

I read the poem as having a subtle tone of defiance toward authority—even of the assignment in question—reminding me of one of my favorite poems, Langston Hughes' "Theme for English B." Sam's poem taps into what I believe is an appropriate response: a healthy disrespect for the institution and a way to talk back to the teacher who assigned the poem. The playful way in which Sam jabs at several central themes of Composition Theory and turns them into his own vision represents his unique, unauthorized engagement with the subject.

The steel footing isn't created or brought to that place in order to kill the cat, and yet the author finds this gruesome, yet oddly humane use for it. The euthanized cat decomposing (de-composition) on the side of the road is Sam's reconfiguration of postmodern deconstruction in relationship to composition. In this poem I see Sam exploring unexpected ways he might use composition theory to serve his and his students' needs and interests rather than the uses I authorize as the teacher. Yet at the same time he "gets it." The line in which he writes about "questioning the answers" is exactly the point of the class and something he demonstrates in this poem. Now, as I begin to watch him make his first foray into teaching, I see that glimmer of mischievousness he brings to his writing classes and the careful distance he remains from the institution, and I am confident that he will be a better teacher for them.

Michael Neal
English

Cat

Sam Renken

—For Mayor John Longo

When you're talking theory
it sometimes seems improbable
to find the answer cut
and dry.

Most of the time,
a cat flat on the road is dead, but that's not theory.
I think it is cut and dry when I lift its still
breathing body to the road's shoulder
and break its calico neck with the steel
footing I found under the railroad tracks.
Though I might tell you time stopped
for a moment, it did not stop the train
on the tracks above me. My theory—
that steel plate dropped on a neck—
only worked in that instant but couldn't
stop the birds singing above the traffic.

Perhaps you should know this is the poem I wrote for Composition
theory.

It's a poem about deconstruction and decomposition,
for a class to help me question the answers
or Proximally develop. Theory is a tool to help me
scaffold, deconstruct, or just line up steel for me
to use like a footing for the railroad ties to follow.
Did you imagine I would use it to break a cat's neck?

Maybe I'm writing
my theory poem
about feline roadkill
euthanasia
because I thought
the cat's broken neck
was definitive,
that my action
and its passing
were cut and dry.

But I drove past that cat today, decomposing,
the traffic didn't even slow down,
most people wheeled by without noticing, and
tomorrow there will always be
another cat.

General Chemistry

One of my persistent goals, and a joy when I can make it work, is finding a way to get my students to "learn outside the box." I had such an opportunity teaching the second course of General Chemistry to Honors students, in which I instituted three activities for class groups: a project on environmental sustainability, a democratic classroom where students "vote" on lecture topics, and construction of multimedia concept maps.

The first evidence that your classroom innovations are having an impact is when the students revolt. Despite detractors that complained that I made the students "do all the work," I pressed on. I knew this approach was outside their comfort zone, but that was the point.

Each student made a PowerPoint® concept map from chapter terms that I provided, then met with their group during class to combine maps for a single group submission. The accompanying slide, by Heather Bandstra, Thomas Beckham, Renee Holland, Caitlin Palazola, Philip Poole, and Harrison Weaver, exemplifies a multimedia concept map. The terms are linked with relationships, and each term is "hot"—it leads to student-created content and possibly to student drawings or learning objects from the Internet (images, simulations, songs, and movies).

Not only did students explore the connections between chapter topics, but they also used their creativity to search for connections to the real world. This example had original art, art from the Internet (removed for copyright reasons), as well as a song about chemistry. The maps attained a multi-dimensional quality that revealed deep student understanding.

In the end the class came around. I have never heard so much discussion about class objectives before, during, and after class! Should I take credit? Was it the concept maps and other group work? I can't say with any certainty, of course, there is no real evidence. Yet I know in my heart that the pedagogies contributed to the course, and perhaps to the students' view of the world. If nothing else I sensed a heightened engagement in class, and that's a goal worthy of repeating.

Jeff Appling
Chemistry

Electrochemistry

*Heather Bandstra, Thomas Beckham, Renee Holland,
Caitlin Palazola, Philip Poole, Harrison Weaver*

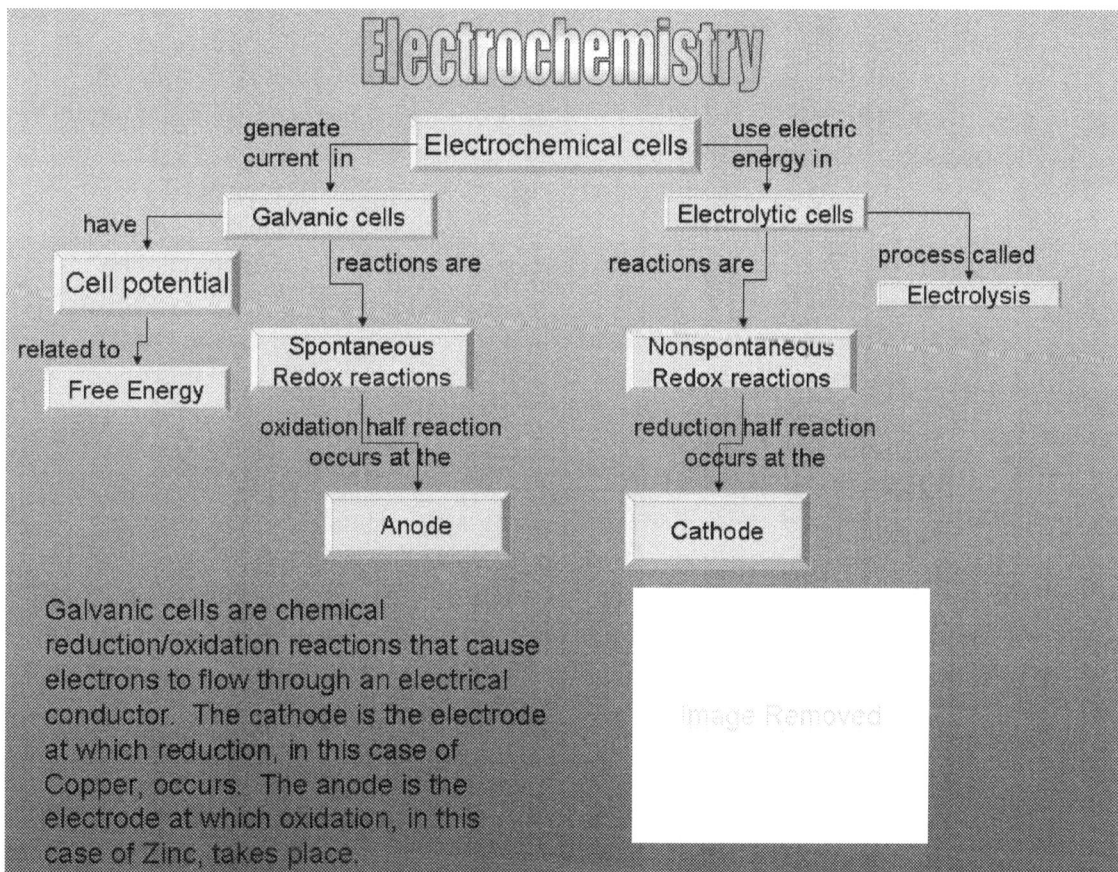

Major Forms of Literature

Perceptive about the way a dead canary suggests the former vibrancy and subsequent misery of Minnie Foster Wright in Susan Glaspell's play *Trifles,* Ashley Hilton demonstrates in her poem "The Canary's Voice" her understanding of drama and of poetry, two of three literary genres we studied in Major Forms of Literature. Ashley dramatizes her own empathy for "Mrs. Wright," whom she describes as "a wife who is tortured her whole married life by an emotionally absent and evil-hearted man." Ashley's poetic sensibility was especially surprising and touching because I never met her or her classmates in this online accelerated summer class.

Students wrote a poem inspired by another literary work we had read plus a reflective essay to explain why they chose the work they revisited and to describe the language and structure of their poems. In her reflection, Ashley wrote, "One of the aspects of the play I like is the moral dilemma." Her poem elicits sympathy for a woman who might have murdered her abusive husband and thus for the women who finds the canary and withholds evidence that might convict Minnie at a time when women could not serve on juries.

Ashley characterizes John Wright as "the devil himself," their home as "hell," and his dreams as "evil" to emphasize her own conviction that Minnie's husband strangled the songbird that had brought color, music, and companionship to their isolated, childless farmhouse: "a fragile yellow child, perches lovingly on her shoulder" and "she rubs its head with a gentle finger . . . / To the place of absent offspring unborn." At the beginning, "A fluttering of wings" appeals to touch, sight, and soft sound. Near the end, "remembrance of fluttering wings" highlights stillness, the canary's neck as well as its cage broken. Ashley's conclusion contrasts more lyrical language earlier and parallels Minnie Wright's situation, incarcerated but removed from her husband's tyranny: "Confined, but finally free." Meaningful in its own right, Ashley's poem demonstrates that she understands the play *Trifles* and the impact of patterns in poetry.

Writing and talking about literature can lead students to critical understanding of the language, context, structure, and meaning of works. When students like Ashley transform that understanding into creative acts of their own, teachers learn that students can communicate knowledge in a variety of ways, including imaginative expression.

Donna Reiss
English

The Canary's Voice

Ashley Hilton

A fluttering of wings creates the cool breeze that brushes her face.
Her eyes close instinctively as if to cherish the soft embrace of disturbed air
That tickles her skin and soul.
The chirping mimics the cooing garbled nonsense of a babe speaking in an
Unknown language.
The bird, a fragile yellow child, perches lovingly on her shoulder
And she rubs its head with a gentle finger—her adopted son
To take the place of absent offspring unborn.
So much love to give.
So little love received from the man who shares her bed.
Her neglected heart, once alive to thrive with life
Is starved for the nourishment of a gentle hand,
A loving touch
Subservient she lives in the hell created inside the lonely farmhouse,
One shared with the devil himself.
Then, with the simple snap of his angry fingers,
She becomes a childless mother again.
Its tiny yellow head—hanging like the leaf of a weeping willow.
She stares with the venom of Eden's serpent
And slips the rope tightly 'round his neck while his evil dreams
Play out their horrors in his deep sleep.
And his head, hanging like the leaf of a weeping willow,
Makes her smile in remembrance of fluttering wings
That tickled her skin and soul.
And now she sits in jail
With no one to make bail.
There for all the world to see,
Confined, but finally free.

College Teaching

As part of their course design project, the students in my graduate-level College Teaching course design a *graphic syllabus*—that is, a flow chart, concept map, or mind map of the topical organization of a course they expect to teach to supplement their text syllabus. The assignment helps them prune non-essential content and tighten their course organization. And it's fun!

J. Christopher Zimmer, a Ph.D. candidate in management information systems and a College Teaching student, created a model graphic syllabus for his hypothetical Database Design and Administration course. He made it genuinely helpful and appealing to undergraduates. His graphic syllabus is clean, simple, easy to follow, and easy to "photograph" into one's mind. Novices who know next to nothing about the subject matter, like many of us, can still understand how he presents and organizes it.

The starting point of Chris' course is relational algebra. He first leads his students through the theoretical foundation of Entity-Relationship (E-R) diagramming, then into physical applications, then through database design and ultimately database building and administration. We can see how the subject matter builds over the weeks, even if the vocabulary still mystifies us. Though we may not know the terrain ahead of us, we at least have a good map.

Chris enhances the utility of his graphic by designating the week in the semester for each topic in the right hand column. To add interest, he varies the shapes of the enclosures, but wisely uses the same shapes for topics on the same level of analysis (for example, "Theoretical Realm" and "Physical Realm," "Build a Database" and "Administer a Database"). He also catches the eye with a few appropriate icons at the top and adds a memorable touch of whimsy in the stick-drawn, happy-faced user.

Chris' design does exactly what a graphic syllabus should do. It gives the "big picture" of his course, a bird's eye view of its structure. In helping the novice make sense of the week-by-week listing, it provides a relatively simple structure that students can borrow to organize and store what they learn.

Linda B. Nilson
Teaching Effectiveness and Innovation

Database Design and Administration
Graphic Syllabus

J. Christopher Zimmer

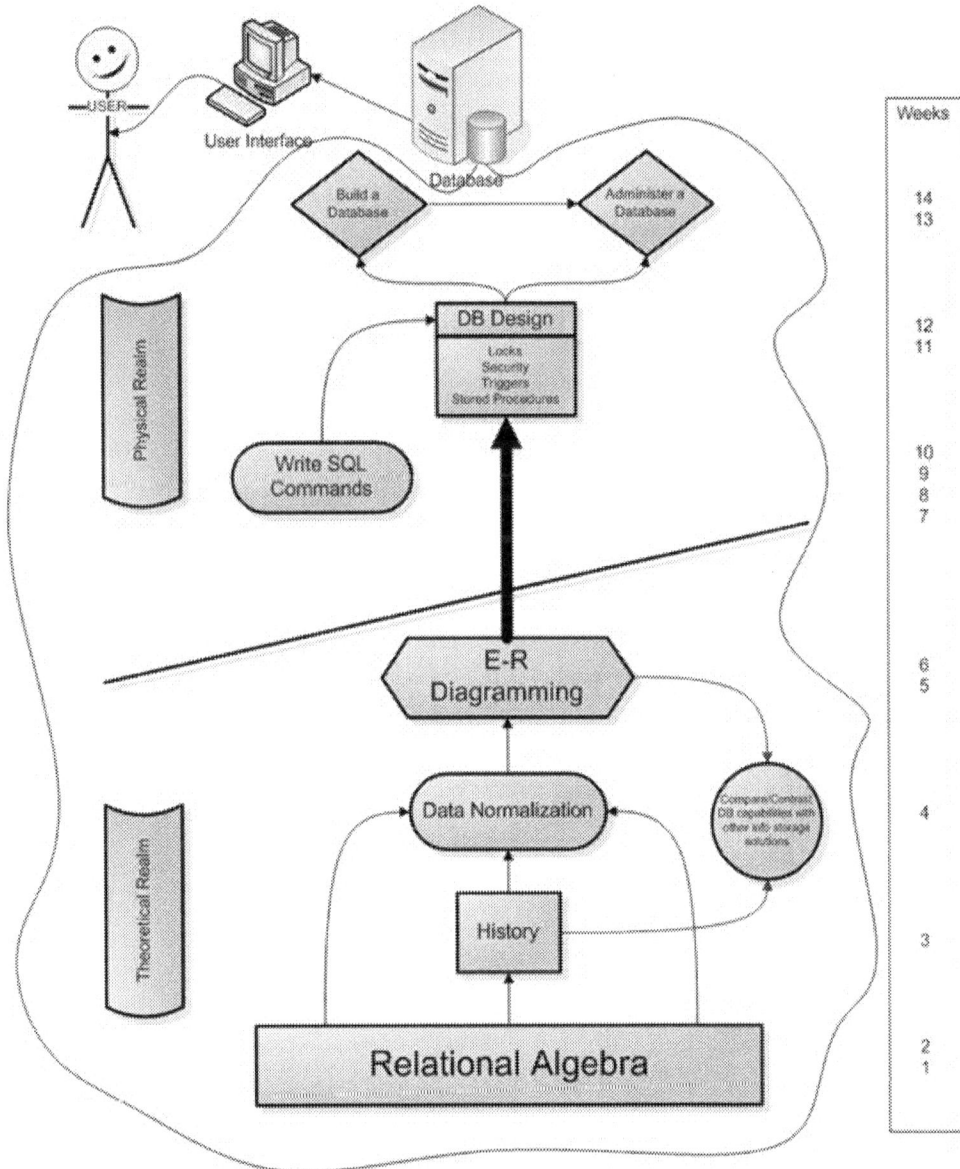

Major Forms of Literature

Karly Grice, a student in my Introduction to Literature class, chose to write a poem in response to Robert Frost's poem "After Apple-Picking." Frost provides the thematic inspiration Karly uses to uniquely compose her own poem, which in a sense strays from a direct response. As Karly explains in her reflection on her writing process: "I wrote "Morning Glory" after reading Frost's poem and thinking about the cycles of life. . . . Instead of focusing on the harvester as Frost did, I made my point of view the thing being harvested, in this case a flower."

What I find so unique and compelling about Karly's poem is how she structures her "Morning Glory" to reflect "the budding and the harvest." "The Budding" stanza reflects the birth of the flower, the innocence of the morning glory's life. Conversely, "The Harvest" stanza reflects the morning glory's last few breaths of life. Karly shares that she uses "light and airy" words to reflect the budding stage and "heavier tones" to "show the weariness of the flower" in the harvesting stage. Ultimately, she explains, each stage shows "an extreme view point, but when taken together the tones balance each other out, much like life." I cannot help but think of William Blake's poetry when I reflect on Karly's process of composing "Morning Glory." There seems to be echoes of the innocence and weariness in each of Karly's stanzas that Blake stresses in his own poetry.

Karly's construction of "The Harvest" stanza remains my favorite aspect of her composition. Karly purposefully juxtaposes the two stanzas, explaining: "This form makes it easy to compare how similar these two very different stages of life are." I love how she pulls the same words from "The Budding" stanza and spins them in such a way that tone and meaning change. "The Harvest" reads as a poignant echo of the previous stanza, which I find effective to the poem's theme.

Emily Benthall Weathers
English

Morning Glory: The Budding and the Harvest

Karly Grice

I open my eyes
for to see the world;
this new place I
call

home.

I unfold
in the
day
and
grow,

closing in,
only for a spell,
as the moon waxes.

Light
rouses me in the morn
as darkness
fades and
a new day
begins.

My life is
a
spring,
it seems,
with no end

Call
me
home,

for the
day

grows
old and night is
closing in.

As the moon waxes,
the soul
light

fades, and

begins

a
slumber

with no end.

Literature for Children

What do you get when you plunk an Industrial Engineering major down in an English course on literature for children and ask her not only to read children's books but to write creatively about her experience of reading children's books? You get "Lindsay's Literature line"—not in a Word document but on an Excel spreadsheet.

The assignment for this poem asked students to write about their relationship to children's books, past, present or future. Lindsay Gauron chose to write about her past, present *and* future relationship to children's books.

I find delight in many aspects of this poem (written by someone who would probably laugh if you accused her of being a poet). I like the ascending gerunds in the first "line" of the poem, the descent into non-literary interests in the second, and the final *flight* of the words completely out of the boundary of the line in the end. This ending suggests, of course, that her newfound interest in reading will survive and grow.

I love this poem because Lindsay comes out of an academic field about which I know almost nothing, and she designed a document that I don't even know how to create. She expressed her ideas with such visual and verbal clarity that she made her classmates gasp.

Michelle H. Martin
English

Lindsay's Literature Line

Lindsay Gauron

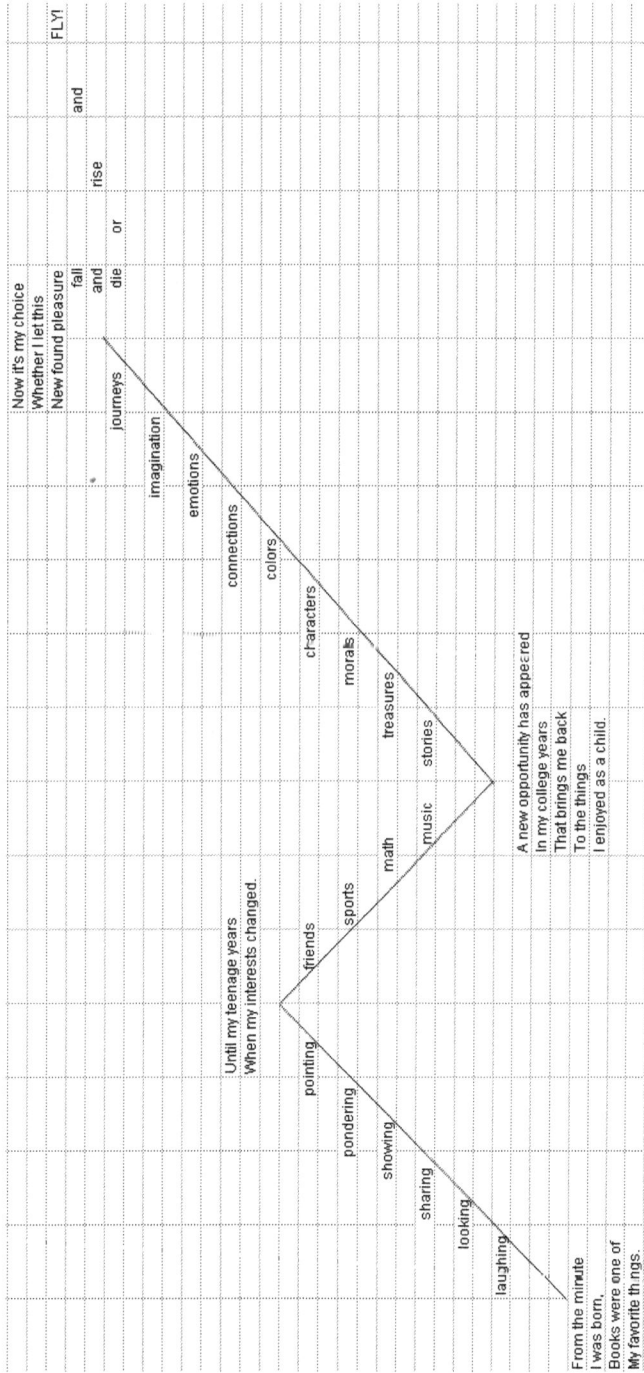

From the minute
I was born,
Books were one of
My favorite things.

laughing
looking
sharing
showing
pondering
pointing

Until my teenage years
When my interests changed.

friends
sports
math
music
stories
treasures
morals
characters
colors
connections
emotions
imagination
journeys

A new opportunity has appeared
In my college years
That brings me back
To the things
I enjoyed as a child.

Now it's my choice
Whether I let this
New found pleasure
fall
and
die
or
rise
and
FLY!

Operations Management

Operations Management classes cover the gamut of planning tools, quantitative models, robotics, and so forth. After we exposed students to theory, a visit to a BMW plant offered a way to show students that classroom "stuff" is relevant to manufacturing. Writing poetry is one way we encourage students to connect their experience of the tour to both classroom theory and their own personal experience. Writing "BMW" seems to free Jeff Henry to playfully and dramatically express himself. Jeff's poem helps us realize the benefits from planning a plant tour and having students express in a creative way what they learn on the plant visit.

Jeff is a serious, no-nonsense student who is not usually as expressive in class as his poem suggests he might be. He demonstrates quite an ability to recognize clearly the components in the plant that relate to course topics but the "student" in him shows him transitioning into the meat of the assignment at his own pace. Often students are awed by the rules imposed on them when they visit industrial plants. Usually there are very good reasons for "no open-toed shoes allowed on the shop floor" and for "wearing safety glasses"—primarily for the visitors safety, but also for the plant's control of liability and meeting insurance regulations. Expecting college students to give up their cell phones without a fuss, not wear sandals, and walk in a single file is unusual, but Jeff's response is an uninterested "I yawn."

However, he quickly progresses from complaining about what he had to do to tour this plant to "let me tell you what I saw." His description of the robots, the assembling of the cars, and the interaction of man and machine allows us to see how he assimilates what he has witnessed. We move from "people are for show," to "robots install," to hearing drivers honk and watching them maneuver, to feeling the musical rhythm of this workplace as a symbiotic "dance of man and machine." The excitement in the last four verses of the poem reassures us that the hassle of planning plant visits is worth every effort required to make them happen. And "BMW" provides us with an enjoyable reading experience and insight into Jeff's lyrical perspective on a plant tour.

Cheryl C. Patterson
Business and Accounting
Furman University

J. Wayne Patterson
Management
Clemson University

BMW

Jeff Henry

We surrender our phones
As we walk past the counter.
Show your ticket, no sandals,
But wear these huge glasses.

What are we doing here?
The headphones jab my ears,
The guide drones on.
I'd rather be napping.

Single file, keep up.
A paint department,
Windows covered. New colors,
So they say. I yawn.

But then . . . cars rumble overhead.
Robots twirl amid firecrackers.
Cars stacked like Lincoln logs,
Flipped and turned and changed.

This is a house of transformation.
Doors hang on racks,
Hoods and bumpers on pallets.
Tires wait for their cars.

The people are for show, right?
An engine passes us,
Driving itself to its car.
Robots install windshield, seat, axle.

The experience isn't Bavarian;
It's surreal. Here, robots weld.
There, drivers honk and maneuver.
A dance of man and machine.

Introduction to Modern Algebra

When I was in college, I had a mathematics professor who would frequently use adjectives such as "great," "beautiful," "exciting," or "elegant" to describe a mathematical result and its proof. Somewhat tongue-in-cheek, but with a personal sense of beauty, he would also name for us some of the theorems he felt were in the "*Top Ten List of Theorems* in God's infinite book." He did this in much the same way that a music lover might talk about the ten greatest symphonies, or a sports buff might talk about the ten greatest baseball players. I also remember that the reaction to the professor's comments by many in the class was, in effect, "They should call for the men in the white jackets to take this fellow away."

Now years later, when I use terms similar to those of my former professor, I wonder if my students are thinking those same men should come take me away. For I deeply believe, as did my professor, that mathematics, in addition to its practicality, is an extremely beautiful subject. I also believe that many students, unfortunately, never experience this beauty. This may be true for more students of lower-level mathematics, but it can also be true for students in upper-level courses.

Modern abstract algebra is an upper-level undergraduate mathematics subject with many great and beautiful theorems and ideas, and I have been privileged to expound on this beauty for many years. While even some students of modern algebra miss its beauty, I find it elating that many do "get it"; that is, perceive the beauty.

Maureen McHugh, the author of the poem on the opposite page, is one student who certainly "got it." The italicized words in Maureen's poem will have a special meaning to students of modern algebra, but they will also have meaning for other readers. Indeed, it will be clear to both groups that Maureen showed that she got it in a special and creative way.

Joel Brawley
Mathematical Sciences

Ode to Math (With Strategically Placed Vocabulary)

Maureen McHugh

Humor me, as I become *reflexive*.
I wish to relate to you the *transformation*
Of my *composition* as a student.
One-to-one, myself and I (the *unique identity*)
I seek to find *mathematical relations*, and to
Generate some *finite order* in my *infinite* mind.

The *field* of *math*, it seems, is *cyclic*,
A *ring mapped onto* itself.
All *classes* appear *equivalent*, a *symmetric group*,
Each *partition* taken as a *subgroup* of the whole.
Outwardly *prime* (*relatively*, at least),
But the *domain* of math is eternal, and
All ideas become *congruen*t; it's just a *function* of time.

This is the *unity* that compels my mind;
This is the beauty that satisfies my soul;
This is *pure*, this is *abstract*, this is the *science* of our world.

This is *math*.

Technical Writing

Chris Workman was a "middle row" student in a technical writing class that was lumbering along. We were working with a client-based project for the local elementary school and some of the students were reluctant to dig into the project, holding back their best time and attention for other projects, other classes. When I mentioned that we would also be writing poems, there was an audible gasp in the room. But I explained that the poems we wrote would be used to add illustration and whimsy to the Grounds Maintenance Manual we were creating for children and their parents and the poems would not be graded. Every student was responsible for a different section of the Grounds Maintenance Manual and had to have a visual representation of that section (a blueprint, a photo, a line drawing). We had three requirements for our poems:

- Poems must be from a point-of-view other than the student's (e.g. a child, a leaf, a hoe, a parent)
- Poems must tell a story
- Poems must incorporate the selected picture either visually or verbally

Around mid-semester, as our project started coming together, we needed our poems to fill out the blank pages of our manual. We shared what had been written so far. One of the sections of the Grounds Maintenance Manual was for a music garden. Chris' poem really caught the attention of the whole class, in part because it was not specifically about children or gardens or play equipment. And the story it told led us in a different direction because it was about the enjoyment of music and words. This poem let us all experience the music garden as a musician would enjoy a guitar. (And, we hoped, would encourage others to want to take care of the music garden.) The class voted for the best poems to be included in the project. "The Guitar" was included in the Grounds Maintenance Manual and voted Best Poem in the class. Chris said, "I've never won anything before, especially not for writing." And after that, Chris took a greater interest in the class; his poem transformed the rhythm of our collaboration and our project. We completed the semester a little lighter on our feet.

Morgan Gresham
English

The Guitar

Chris Workman

A wooden
Body with
Metal strings
Are what
It is
Made
Of, a
Simple
Design
That in
Skilled
Hands
Has the
Power
To move
And inspire those who hear
The music that comes from within
Not only the guitar but the person playing
It. Many use this instrument as an outlet
Letting all of their emotions flow through
Their fingers to the strings like water
From a faucet. Millions are
Made each year no two alike,
Each possessing a sound all its own.
Whether electric or a simple acoustic the joy
of playing simple chord progressions or bars from
A favorite song is the same. The escape from the
Everyday world is the same as you forget about the
Events of the day and simply focus on the notes
Being played and the sounds coming
From the guitar.

Studies in Environmental Science, Law, and Policy

This course enhances the scientific and technical learning of students through a shift in viewpoint. Geology majors, Civil Engineers, Wildlife Biologists, Packaging Science majors learn how their knowledge and data fit into the broader societal picture where the American legal system and policy makers work with their science. For me, the wisdom of the ancients and a liberal arts background had a voice "out there in the world" and in a fact-intensive field.

My classes participate in the Poetry Across the Curriculum project. And Jason Meadows, a Sophomore Geology major, amazed his classmates and professors with his "Of Carrots and Sticks," a structured, sometimes-rhyming poem addressing the legal/regulatory policies of incentives ("carrots"), and penalties ("sticks"). As a fellow student exclaimed, "This is a Dead Poets Society quality poem."

Playful and engaging, with a stream-of-consciousness flow, Jason's poem became the benchmark for every subsequent poetry assignment. The School of the Environment sent the poem around its listserv, as did the College of Engineering and Science. Poetry has allowed me to give bright science and technology majors an opportunity to try their hand at a skill once universally taught. In this way all students and teachers participate in a liberal arts education for undergraduates.

Margaret Louise Thompson
Environmental Engineering and Science

Of Carrots and Sticks: Reflections on Environmental Policy

Jason Bryan Meadows

Some shout "Only carrots!"
Others cry "Only sticks!"
And still there are those who ask for "Neither!"
    (to whom I say "Get Real!")
Alas! If the people were smart
I would give them only carrots
Or, if stubborn and cattle, only sticks
But in my experience they are both
And such requires a mix.

For remember:
When they are big,
    carrots are of poorer quality
When they are big,
    sticks frighten more
When they are small,
    carrots are more alluring
When they are small,
    sticks are called twigs

Wise mothers say,
"Eat your carrots!"
    and
"Don't play with sticks!"
Both to the benefit of your eyes
So to see with clear vision,
My own wisdom is this:
Carrots are the measure of a gem
    take them while you can
On the far side of sticks is Hades
    avoid them while you can.

President's Seminar

As university faculty, we frequently deal with students who are new not just to the school but to the region. "Dixieland Delight and Southern Comfort" was submitted as part of a sequence of poems for a capstone course known at Clemson as "The President's Seminar." The interdisciplinary course brought together fifteen students and eight faculty to consider the function of setting in a number of art forms and disciplines. The basic text for the course was Eudora Welty's great essay "Place in Fiction" which explains both the technical and thematic part of setting in works of art in general.

We found it particularly interesting that our topic dove-tailed so tightly with the situation of Angelina Oberdan who had come to Clemson from St. Louis. She told us that, as part of her adjustment to her new place, she had to explain to friends in Missouri that she was okay in, and about, the South. Thus this poem.

We found it interesting, too, that she pursued the theoretical or academic implications of place in areas such as architecture, poetry, film, theatre, music; then she applied those theories and ideas to her own personal and immediate situation; and then she turned back to an artistic expression as she produced her poems, identifying in a variety of ways the elements of her place. In effect, we like to think, aesthetic experience informed Angelina's personal situation and then generated more of the aesthetic.

James F. Barker
Architecture
President, Clemson University

Bill Koon
English

Dixieland Delight and Southern Comfort

Angelina Oberdan

We are Southerners in seersucker suits
sipping sweet tea on the front porch
as the sun sets over the Blue Ridge Mountains.
This is God's country and we live by the Bible,
love our fried chicken, football and NASCAR.
We are slow talkers and strong drinkers:
gentlemen and sweet southern belles—
tailgating alumni who bet on horse races.
This is our place—Dixieland delight and
southern comfort sleeping soundly
to the twanging lullaby of a southern accent.

Math Out of the Box

Why are we discussing writing in a mathematics curriculum? Because writing is a process that allows students to reflect on their own understanding—in any content area. In mathematics, writing is not simply a way to display what is known, but a way to acquire what is not yet known.

Math Out of the Box is a research and development project at Clemson University in which a team of professors, mathematics specialists, and teachers work together to produce an inquiry-based mathematics curriculum for kindergarten through fifth grade. The communication model generates opportunities for written exploration of mathematical concepts. In this environment students have the freedom to take risks so that verbal and written communication can occur and develop.

One strategy incorporated into the lessons of the curriculum is a task called "Home Connections" in which families work together to solve problems. Third-grader Levi Owens and his family wrote "All About Our Pattern," which followed classroom work where repeating patterns were analyzed, described, and represented in a variety of ways.

The recognition of patterns is an important mathematics skill because patterns are all around us in nature, architecture, poetry, and our number system. Understanding of patterns in elementary grades helps students with algebra and other concepts later in school.

Levi's family was challenged to work together to find architectural patterns in their neighborhood. They were instructed to choose a favorite place that they could draw and describe. Many of South Carolina's villages formed around a textile mill. In the early days of these villages, housing for the workers was provided by the mills. Levi and his family recognized the fantastic architecture in the historic town of Ninety Six where they live.

As described in the text above his illustration, Levi has made a powerful connection between mathematics and the "mill village houses" on his street. Thinking about patterns mathematically is a tool that Levi will now be able to apply to other situations in math class, other subject areas, and his world.

Bill Moss
Mathematical Sciences

Dot Moss
Mathematical Sciences

All About Our Pattern

Levi Owens
Ninety Six Elementary School

Math Out of the Box

Home Connection 4   Levi

All About Our Pattern Our favorite architectural Pattern is in the mill village houses on the street we live on. The Porches are diffent every third house. The first two have banisters then the third house hasia brick M Shape. It keeps this Pattern all the way down the street.

Forms of Literature

When I first read Lauren Barnett's poem and reflection, it unsettled me. Lauren presents me with a new way of reading "The River-Merchant's Wife: A Letter" by Ezra Pound. Lauren enrolled in my Forms of Literature class, where I spend a significant amount of time discussing poetry. Pound's poem is one of the poems we evaluate. Usually, I teach this poem from the perspective of a love poem where the speaker gradually falls in love with her husband *after* their arranged marriage, which is quite different from how we Westerners are accustomed to falling in love. At the end of the poetry section, I generally ask the students to write a poem in response to one of the poems we studied and then to write a brief reflection on their writing process.

I viewed Pound's poem only through the lens of a beautiful Eastern love poem. When I looked at the poem through Lauren's lens, I caught another perspective. I saw how the world of the speaker was quite limited, especially in comparison to the world of a twenty-first century, Western twenty-something. Lauren's reading of "The River-Merchant's Wife" will always affect my own reading and teaching of the poem because it contrasts two very different interpretations.

Lauren chose to respond to Pound's poem by writing directly to the speaker of the poem. She explained her perspective by stating, "When I read Ezra Pound's 'The River-Merchant's Wife,' it annoyed me that the wife has led such an unfulfilling life. She was forced to marry someone that she did not love, which made her miserable for a while. Then, her misery turned to desperation and obsession. She cannot stand to be without him, which is pathetic. Pound uses phrases like 'sorrowful,' 'dragged your feet,' 'too deep to clear,' and 'they hurt me' to show the wife's state of being."

I am also interested in how Lauren talks about writing her poem: "I tried to include some poetic techniques . . . the last four lines of the second, third, and fourth stanzas begin with a verb to show that life is meant to be participated in. The first stanza gives the background for the poem. Each line in the second stanza has six syllables, the third has five syllables, and the fourth has four syllables. The purpose of this decreasing order is to narrow the poem down to the last line which is the climax of the poem."

Lauren reads Pound's poem as a passive text, and therefore wishes to make her own poem active by emphasizing action verbs "to show that life is meant to be participated in." She purposefully structures each stanza to accentuate her final stanza, and, in turn, defining what she believes it means to truly live.

Emily Benthall Weathers
English

My Life: A Response to "The River-Merchant's Wife"

Lauren Barnett

In ten million minutes I have
    Witnessed a shooting star
    Watched some frisky dolphins
    Learned from many mistakes
    Believed in miracles

In one hundred thousand hours I have
    Walked by glistening waves
    Loved some and lost some
    Traveled in Europe
    Rallied for pro-life

In seven thousand days I have
    Been a catholic
    Gone to college
    Ridden bareback
    Prayed with the pope

In twenty years
    I have lived.

Food Technology Product Development

In this course teams use a hands-on research and development approach to create new food concepts. My hope is that by teaming students with various levels of technical experience, culinary skills, and diverse personalities we can accurately mimic the R & D process in industry. Teams begin the project with brainstorming—essential as it engages team members with respect to trends and changing views. Members focus on key questions such as: Can we make this new product? Will the customer buy it?

Class teams are allowed to create any new food concept and throughout the semester they cook, test, and evaluate their creations. What I particularly like about this project is that each team follows the "Driving New Products to Market" model that includes multiple steps of review and analysis.

The "Jala-Mango" team with Michael Ryan, Brad Ballieu, Abel Caballero, Heather Johnson, and Rachel Yost honed in on a popular flavor bundle. The course emphasized the stage-gate method of product development, where the product could have been "killed" at any time, leaving the students to start over with a new product. But they persevered. The students thus demonstrated the professionalism of a research and development team, an important attitude that I try to cultivate in my students.

The team decided to focus on two consumer benefits, convenience and flavor. The convenience of large vegetable pieces, which are rarely used in commercial sauces, reduces the need for consumers to chop vegetables at home. The team also tested formulations and textures to create the optimal preparation and presentation attributes for this product, which was then entered in a food ingredient company competition. The judging criteria for the contest centered on flavor, technical feasibility, texture, appearance, nutrition profile, and market potential. Ultimately their new sweet and sour jalapeno-flavored sauce won a large cash prize, not only validating the students' efforts, but also providing them with an exposure to industry that traditional coursework rarely provides.

As a teacher I learned that the project guideline is an important base for evaluation. However, of greater importance are the team dynamics and timely availability of tools for production, which already has me thinking about new ways to provide my students with even more realistic ways to learn about the workplace.

Marge Condrasky
Food Science and Human Nutrition

Jala-Mango

Brad Ballieu, Abel Caballero, Heather Johnson, Michael Ryan, Rachel Yost

Writing Architecture

As part of a collaborative writing course between Clemson's English and architecture departments, architecture professor Kemp Mooney and I created an assignment that asked students to narrate an encounter with the building they were designing. Professor Mooney, in his third-year design studio, emphasizes an inhabitant's experience of a building. The writing assignment was a creative one, but the primary and secondary research and the poetry-writing that led up to the main project reinforced for me the connection between creativity and critical thinking.

As background for writing about their own buildings, we read architect Daniel Libeskind's writing about his design for the Jewish Museum in Berlin. We studied slides of the museum, an ideal method of researching the project, since Libeskind thinks of his building as a text that uses language and metaphor to tell a story. The slides, taken by one of the students on a trip to Berlin, showed that visitors to the museum don't merely observe artifacts in a building; the experience of the building *is* the artifact. The building itself is inscribed with meaning that took shape through the architect's experience of a variety of texts, including an opera, the inscriptions in his own passport, the pages of a Berlin guidebook, the baroque museum adjacent to the museum site, and a memorial book containing the names of Jews killed in the Holocaust. Libeskind's writing, in word choices and content, connotes the building's language and content.

After studying the museum, students wrote poems in which buildings speak. In Stevyn Buie's poem, the Holocaust museum becomes a body with a shape that stands, reclines, rests. It has life, individuality, and it relates to people. It knows disenfranchisement and recognizes itself as a manifestation of the architect's mind, as perhaps even a sideshow.

This exploration of metaphor created a space for students to think intuitively about their own projects. Writing the poem allowed students to consciously integrate language into their conceptual processes. It also showed that buildings have a voice and power to shape and create meaning. By creating a metaphor between the language of poetry and the language of architecture, this assignment fostered creative, critical thinking.

Jennie Wakefield
English

Self Reflection of the Holocaust Museum

Stevyn Buie

Standing here amongst the rest of the city buildings . . . or . . . am I lying
    down?
Gently resting upon green landscape
I feel ostracized from the rest of the blocks around me
Part of me loves my individuality,
My other part hates the stares and scrutiny
Day to day people roam through my interior . . .
Looking, traveling, thinking of years long gone

The visitors make me feel alive
Upon and at their appreciation and awe I thrive
The best of the best; a wonderful work
I hold memories, valuables with endless worth.
Some say I'm what draws the people here
And not the pain of a race of people who shed many tears
I house uniqueness unlike any of those around me
I'm so thankful that, somewhere in his great mind, Libeskind, found me

But still I feel the stares from human pupils
To some I'm like a mistake . . . I sense the skeptics' stares
So I remain here now as an object of much conversation
Fulfilling my purpose . . . whatever it may be for whomever it may be
The ins and outs of me constantly scrutinized
The life of a famous building . . .

Art with Computer

In teaching art we often use the description "visual poetry," though the meaning of the phrase may have nothing to do with words. In this context, visual poetry refers to visual elements working so well with one another that they "sing."

I teach our art and design students the use of the computer as a professional and creative tool. I introduce software packages that use vector and bitmap graphics, typographic, and many other digital tools and concepts. The poetry writing was part of an assignment on vector graphics combined with typography. The students were to compose their own poetry and graphics, making use of the tools in the software package.

Brian Walker's academic major was graphic communications, which prepares students for the highly technical world of the printing industry. He was a serious, motivated student with a deep interest in music.

Brian's image combines a delicate balance of looseness and control. He shows a high degree of spontaneity, with some marks resembling hand-work while others use the computer's own precise language. Although created as part of an exercise to learn the software, the end product is much more than a technical exercise. Brian's expressive use of various forms of mark-making and the repetitions of type and lines gives the work a strong rhythm of the joys of free roaming, with a hint of fear of losing control.

Brian's work went beyond my expectations of the assignment. Yet on the other hand, this, after all, is an art class, where technical commands are only means and artistic and personal expressions instead are the goals. This is one case where a student work did "sing."

Sam Wang

Art

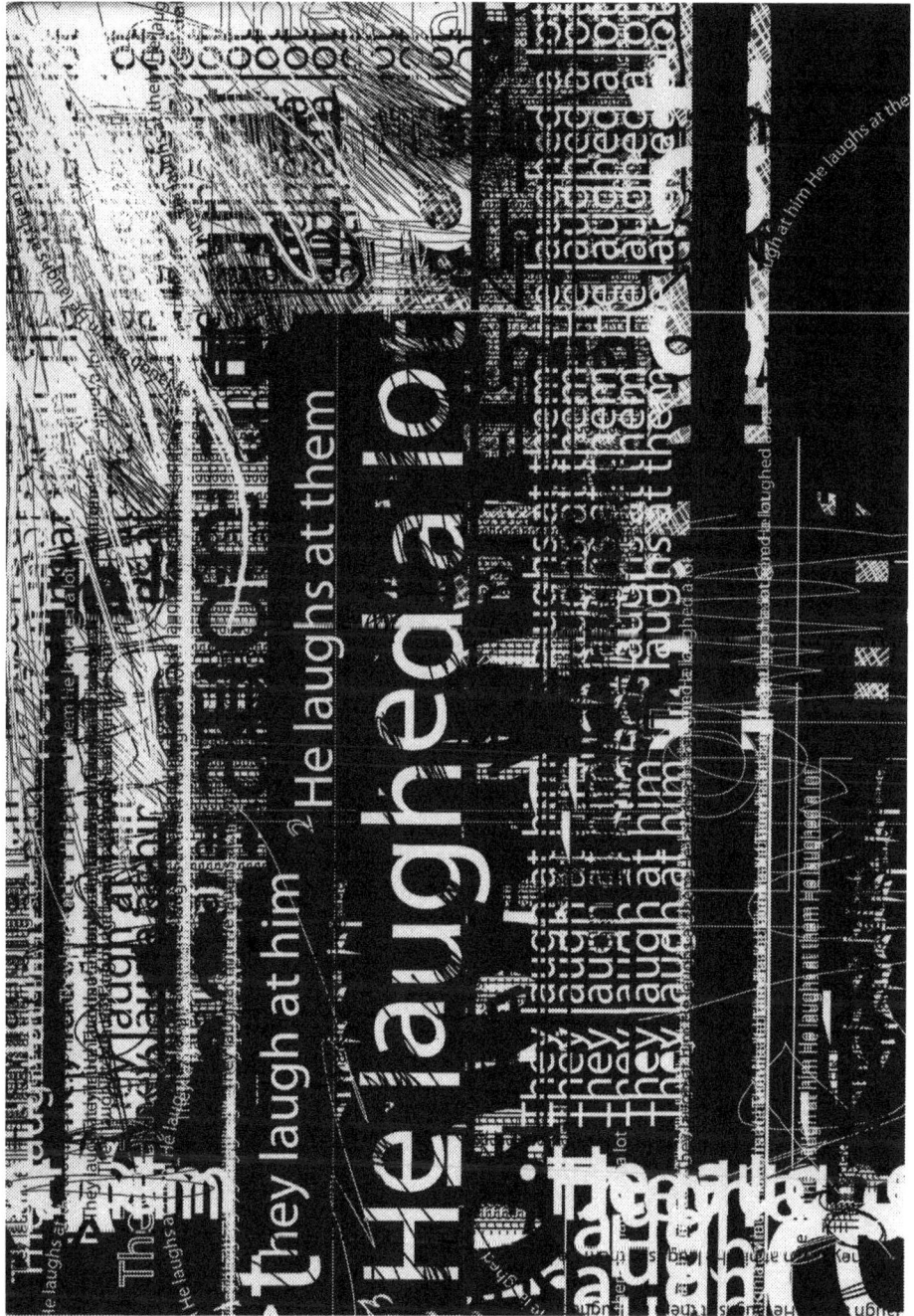

They Laughed at Him

Brian Walker

Business Statistics

On a recent trip to the beach, we discussed Bo Gillooly's poem as a most remarkable and ingenious response to an assignment that most other students had treated in a sterile—just the facts—à la Dragnet—manner. Analysis of variance and related procedures provided the focus for this assignment, and students were to write a poem focusing either on a specific statistical procedure or a collage of the concepts. Bo picked the latter and very effectively covered virtually all the material in two chapters of the textbook, giving a creative, playful, and accurate account of how he saw the various concepts fitting together.

While the poem will not cause the practice of statistical analysis to change dramatically, the insight Bo expresses is a comfort to even the most cold-hearted statistics professor. Bo was alert in class, but he was probably one of the last people to voluntarily answer or further a discussion. But give him this assignment, and he put the subject matter to life in a surprising and entertaining way. Neither of us can figure out how he selected the Gettysburg Address to plug in the statistical concepts the way he did.

As we discussed Bo's poem, we almost felt like he was drawing a parallel to the enduring quality of the Gettysburg Address to the application of statistics. Is that a stretch for a student in a statistics class, or what? The ease with which he accomplished the goal of the assignment was truly remarkable. As awkward as he may have felt with this assignment, or even in doing the statistical analysis, you'd never guess it from his completed work. Bo's freedom to write in the form of a poem allowed him to show us that he saw the big picture clearly and that is every teacher's goal in a required course.

We agreed that poems like this one come along all too rarely but when they do they are worth the wait. As Bo so skillfully illustrated, creative responses to unusual assignments that appear routine can have an enduring quality of their own.

J. Wayne Patterson
Management
Clemson University

Cheryl C. Patterson
Business and Accounting
Furman University

Region of Rejection: Gettysburg Address Revisited

Bo Gillooly

Four score and seven years ago,
our Tukey brought forth on this subject a new formula
conceived in the Studentized range,
and dedicated to the proposition
that all pairs' two corresponding population means are not equal.

Now we are engaged in a great Bartlett's Test,
testing whether that variance, or any other variance,
independent and normal, can long endure.

We are met on a great battlefield between two mighty tests.
We have come to dedicate a portion of the Wilcoxon Rank Sum field,
as a final resting place for those who are ranked and independent,
and another field to ranked and non-normal samples,
who gave their lives so that Kruskal-Wallis might live.

It is altogether fitting and proper that we should do this.
But, in a larger sense we can not forget General Friedman,
for we cannot consecrate a whole block without this fallen comrade,
and so we hallow this statistical ground, as ANOVA, sum of squares, a
    treatment.

Advanced Technical Writing

To feature a bus schedule as a creative project may seem to be an unusual choice but this is one document that stands out for me. My class took on the challenge of encouraging low-income women of color to go for free breast and cervical cancer screenings at the Joseph F. Sullivan Center for Nursing and Wellness on campus. While women in the class could interview women and do other contingent tasks, the men in the class needed a different project that would not involve questioning women about their bodies. During the interviews, we noticed that one reason these women did not come into the Center was that parking and transportation were problematic. Two male students, Ed Ballew and Sharif Ewees, decided that they would provide a more user-friendly schedule for the free bus system.

Creative problem solving is a main component of my service-learning classes. Students discovered on their own the truism that low-income people often miss opportunities because of a lack of basic resources like transportation. When other more obvious solutions were not available to them, Ed and Sharif designed and tested a bus schedule that showed an easier way to reach the Center. The color-coding of time slots to match the directions of bus travel and the sun/moon symbols enhanced comprehension. The students were creative in their research methods: interviewing the head of the bus system, taking multiple schedules to the women and asking them which ones they preferred, making them a part of the project, too.

Researching such projects, students see the world with "new" eyes, especially when they have grown up in somewhat privileged environments. In their communities, low-income people were present but not visible to them. When students meet people in contexts other than their own, they start making breakthroughs in their thinking. Rather than preach at students, I let the situations present the problems.

I admire the creativity of the young men who wanted to contribute to the project without offending our target audience. Their conscientiousness was impressive. This project taught me to challenge students with difficult problems and new audiences, trusting them to find creative solutions, rather than scripting every project detail for them.

Barbara Heifferon
English

Purple Route (Bus Schedule)

Ed Ballew, Sharif Ewees

Purple Route (D) Northeast Residential

Service from C-1 Lot or P-1 Lot on request only

All times are departures except those outlined in red

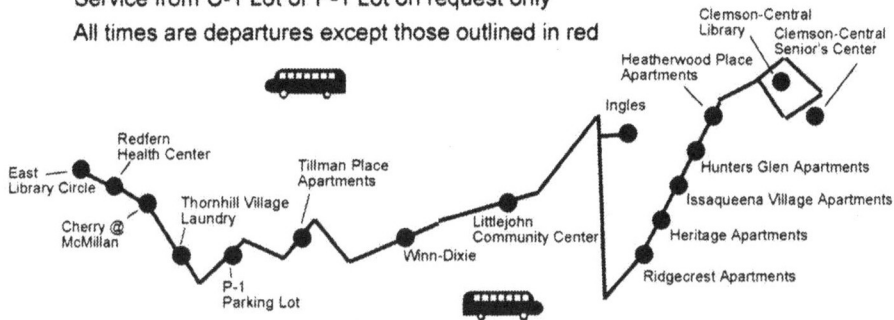

Monday/Wednesday/Friday Service

Clem-Central Senior Center	7:18	8:25	8:28	9:30	9:33	10:25	10:28	11:40	11:43	12:45	12:48		1:50	1:53	2:56	2:58	4:00	4:01	5:25
Apartments on Issaqueena Trl	7:20	8:19	8:30	9:24	9:35	10:29	10:40	11:34	11:45	12:39	12:50		1:44	1:55	2:49	3:00	3:54	4:03	5:19
Ingles		7:25	8:16	8:35	9:21	9:40	10:26	10:45	11:31	11:50	12:36	12:55	1:41	2:00	2:46	3:05	3:51	4:06	5:16
Littlejohn CC		7:28	8:13	8:38	9:18	9:43	10:23	10:48	11:28	11:53	12:33	12:58	1:38	2:03	2:43	3:08	3:48	4:11	5:13
Winn-Dixie		7:30	8:11	8:40	9:16	9:45	10:21	10:50	11:26	11:55	12:31	1:00	1:36	2:05	2:41	3:10	3:46	4:13	5:11
Tillman Place		7:34	8:06	8:44	9:11	9:49	10:16	10:54	11:21	11:59	12:26	1:04	1:31	2:09	2:36	3:14	3:41	4:17	5:06
Thornhill Village		7:43	8:02	8:48	9:07	9:53	10:12	10:58	11:17	12:03	12:22	1:08	1:27	2:13	2:32	3:18	3:37	4:21	5:02
East Library		7:48	8:00	8:51	9:05	9:56	10:10	11:01	11:15	12:06	12:20	1:11	1:25	2:16	2:30	3:21	3:35	4:24	5:00

Tuesday/Thursday Service

Clem-Central Senior Center	7:18	8:25	8:53	9:55	10:23	11:25	11:53	12:55	1:23	2:25	2:23	3:55	4:01	5:25	
Apartments on Issaqueena Trl	7:20	8:19	8:55	9:49	10:25	11:19	11:55	12:49	1:25	2:19	2:25	3:49	4:03	5:19	
Ingles		7:25	8:16	9:00	9:46	10:30	11:16	12:00	12:46	1:30	2:16	2:30	3:46	4:08	5:16
Littlejohn CC		7:28	8:13	9:03	9:43	10:33	11:13	12:03	12:43	1:33	2:13	2:33	3:43	4:11	5:13
Winn-Dixie		7:30	8:11	9:05	9:41	10:35	11:11	12:05	12:41	1:35	2:11	2:35	3:41	4:13	5:11
Tillman Place		7:34	8:06	9:09	9:36	10:39	11:06	12:09	12:36	1:39	2:06	2:39	3:36	4:17	5:06
Thornhill Village		7:43	8:02	9:13	9:32	10:43	11:02	12:13	12:32	1:43	2:02	2:43	3:32	4:21	5:02
East Library		7:46	8:00	9:16	9:30	10:46	11:00	12:16	12:30	1:46	2:00	2:46	3:30	4:24	5:00

Knowledge Development in Advanced Nursing Practice

"Knowing" in nursing refers to ways of perceiving and understanding the self and the world. Knowing is a dynamic process. In my nursing theory course we examine four patterns of knowing in nursing: empirics, ethics, aesthetics and personal knowing. Poetry writing helps my students understand aesthetic knowing, which makes it possible to move beyond the surface to sense the meaning of some moment and connect with the depths of human experience (sickness, grief, recovery, birth). Aesthetic knowing in practice is expressed in actions, attitude, narrative and interactions of the nurse in relation to others. It is also formally expressed in art forms such as poetry. Students in my class were asked to write a poem that described the "lived" experience of nursing and the experience of health and illness.

Lucy Barnett's poem captured the artistry of nursing as she described the experience of caring for a person with Alzheimer's disease. The poem captured the nurse in the interaction of caring: being, relating (personally, interpersonally) and doing (actions and decision making). Through her poem I entered into a place of hurt and pain, sharing the brokenness, confusion and anguish of Alzheimer's. I felt Lucy's compassion as the poem challenged the reader to mourn with those who suffer loneliness. Lucy was as vulnerable and powerless as her patient. Compassion means full immersion in the condition of being human. In this poem Lucy's personal self and professional self are inextricably intertwined and define her practice of nursing.

I also sensed that Lucy was suffering an agonizing vulnerability because, as so often happens in the practice of nursing, there was a collision of the personal self's compassion and tenderness with the professional self's conscience and sense of duty to care for patients. I sensed the strain in providing compassionate care despite her own human vulnerability to the hurts of this patient. I worried about her need for replenishment of physical, mental and spiritual energy.

What emerged from this poem was the portrait of a nurse who is very human with a personal side that molds and influences her perceptions of self as a nurse, the way she practices and how she perceives patients.

Bonnie Holaday
Family and Neighborhood Life

Alone She Sits in Her Chair

Deborah Lucy Barnett

Alone she sits in her chair
The place she stays, I lead her there
She watches the world untouched by her voice
She sits in her chair but not by choice

Words no longer pass her lips
As the day drags on, her mind slips
Into a world not of her choosing
A world where her essence she is losing

Names with faces no longer match
Thoughts fly by she can't seem to catch
Words for things she can no longer name
Things seem different nothing's the same

Time for rounds it's time to eat
I lead her to the dining seat
Forks and spoons are no longer needed
She uses her hands and eats unheeded

Unaware of those who sit nearby
Unfazed by my words or heavy sigh
I wipe her face and touch her hair
I lead her back to her lonely chair

Outdoor Recreation Resources
Management and Planning

Some students don't like surprises in their coursework. Moans always erupt from some students when I announce the small additional assignment a week or so after the start of class: write a poem that reflects the subject matter of the course. A cacophony of questions fills the small room. "A poem . . . what kind of poem? How long must it be? Does it have to rhyme? Why must I read it to the class? What *is* the subject matter of the course anyway?"

I've learned that some students don't like an additional challenge. In their minds, it's unfair and inexcusable for faculty to add work not previously included on the syllabus. Thus, they interrogate me until I decide to throw up my hands indicating I've heard enough and to close the discussion. I tell them to have fun with the assignment. I reassure them it will not be graded based on its quality or the number of lines, but a class participation grade is clearly indicated in the syllabus. So, their participation is not required, but it is remembered. Now assured the assignment is not a threat to the status quo, the students calm down and display some interest in attempting the task, as evidenced by the few smiles and now low chatter and laughter present.

Crayton Pruitt's poem arrived the third time I tried the assignment and is one of my favorite renditions of the course subject matter. Crayton indicates that he has an acute interest and concern for the natural environment, which he metaphorically humanizes with references to nature's intricate beauty that is often taken for granted. He entreats the reader to note the beauty, though he does not specifically identify the features he enjoys the most, leaving readers to see nature's beauty through their own eyes. Lastly, he challenges all of us, who recognize the beauty in nature, to protect it from the forces that would degrade it. Such insight expressed so poetically is truly a breath of fresh air. (And, the poem even rhymes!)

Grant Cunningham
Planning & Landscape Architecture

True Beauty in the Eyes of the Beholder

Crayton Pruitt

She catches me off guard, all by surprise;
Her beauty is something, that is truly, more than meets the eyes.
She's there all day, holding in her grace;
Most days it's subtle; it's the others that one must truly embrace.
I find myself wondering, about the mystery within;
One day to presume the average, and then be caught by her beauty again.
Her value we must hold in highest regard;
For if we don't, her true beauty will become clearly marred.
One may ask how she keeps herself in disguise;
Just to bloom with her true beauty, in front of our eyes.
The wild thing is our love is not to last;
While just a little more care would get her past.
I will save you! We would all like to cry;
However, each of us witnesses her slow death, with a turned eye.
It is nature, I speak of, and how she makes us feel;
Yet with little changes her future is merely surreal.
So love her each day, and hold your feelings true;
We will keep her trees green, and her waters so blue.

Legal Issues & Instructional Materials Development

Online learning is an increasingly popular tool for reaching non-traditional students. As part of an online Masters Degree program at Clemson, we implemented a cooperative activity between two graduate-level courses. Our students were geographically dispersed executives from the Boys and Girls Clubs of America (BGCA) who were paired together on a project that blended theory and application related to educating individuals about legal issues in large organizations. The students developed training websites on legal issues which BGCA employees may encounter in their clubs.

From an instructional perspective, we taught the students about various design issues fundamental to visual communication for training websites. Each team brainstormed via online discourse about effective colors, layouts and images, and creative delivery of instructional concepts. Our students explored techniques such as online case studies, role-playing, and scavenger hunts.

Mike Marnin and John Pham produced the site entitled Opening Doors to a Safer Club. The homepage from their site is shown here. In addition to the appealing graphic design of the homepage, including children opening doors to a club, Mike and John incorporated innovative instructional tools into the structure of their site. These include "Judge for Yourself," which provides real-life cases where the learner responds to a specific set of thought-provoking questions that raise legal questions about club safety. Another tool, "Cruise a Club," included images of club facilities that featured various safety hazards for the learner to identify. Both of these tools are educationally robust in that they use interactive concepts requiring the learner to engage in higher-order thinking activities that teach the desired legal objectives. All of the teams eventually shared their final work in an online forum through which constructive feedback was provided via online peer assessment.

Many of Mike and John's ideas were such fine examples of creativity and effective use of design that we have incorporated them into our teaching for subsequent courses, demonstrating once again the synergy that can occur between teachers and students when we use creative approaches to learning. We have found that linking skills-based content with theoretical issues, through the use of learning communities, raises the overall level of student learning and creativity.

K. Dale Layfield
Biological Sciences
Clemson University

Bruce Berger
Business Administration and Law
Western Carolina University

Opening Doors to a Safer Club

Mike Marnin
John Pham

Six-Legged Science

In the 12 years since I began asking my students to generate a creative project, I have never been disappointed with their efforts. The only guidelines students receive about these assignments are that the result must be related to Entomology, that it must be scientifically accurate (or if poetic license is taken, then the reality needs to be explained), and the student has to tell me what they have learned. Often students express some concern that they are not creative. In the end, however, creativity has not been a problem.

One of the best outcomes of the assignment is that as students share their work, each in their turn is showcased and rewarded by the other students' enjoyment of their work. I like to think that I connect with students on a personal level, but every time a student surprises me with their work, I realize I have much to learn before I truly connect with them. While their projects are not intended to be serious reflections of their lives, just having a small window into their creative spirit makes me conscious of the complexity of each individual.

The poem on termites by Mike Collins represents one of my surprises, in no small part because Mike is a 6'4" Clemson University football player. Don't get me wrong; Mike is also a good student. He readily asks questions and is often the one who answers my questions to the class. He is engaged with his education. Every indication is that he will excel at his chosen profession of working in criminal justice. He is affable, laughs easily, and manages to not intimidate anyone with his large frame. Many students come into an introductory Entomology course with a negative view of most insects, especially destructive species like termites. The fact that Mike could see the world from the termite's point of view was a delightful departure.

So once again I was stopped in my tracks and made conscious of how little I know about my students. Each semester, I learn a little more.

Pat Zungoli
Entomology, Soils, and Plant Sciences

I Am Worker Termite; Hear Me Roar!

Michael Collins

Now look,
We've been very patient with you up-right
and tall,
But enough is enough;
Now its time to brawl.

Look, we have bosses
That need to be fed.
The only thing about it,
They wear crowns and tiaras on their heads.

Yes King and Queen Isoptera
Need their food
So excuse me
If I am just a little rude.

We were nice enough
To live in the woods
But here you come
Building your fancy neighborhoods.

You then take away
That which we eat
Please sit down;
Here you go take a seat.

Oh, you can't
I forgot, I had to eat the chair
Because when I went to feed
Nothing else was there.

So you see the dilemma
That you humans obviously cause?
Forcing us to eat
Your furniture, books and walls.

It is not our fault
Just so you know.
It is just like being cold,
Whenever there is snow.

It is just
A logical order of events;
We're there, you come, we feed,
And you apply defense.

You try to stop us
With your intellectual parts
But, we are social insects
And we too have smarts.

Don't be fooled by the fact
That some us have no eyes.
We see what you are doing.
It is no surprise.

You're trying to destroy our colonies
With your chemicals and structural design
You're trying to slaughter us
As if we were swine.

But we will not go peacefully
Or without a fight

We're not out of mind
Or out of sight.

Here is an idea
One that might work out
And put an end
To this long and hard fought bout.

You take us as pets
And give us what we need;
And we won't consider your possessions
When it is time for us to feed.

Technical Writing

As part of a multi-semester project in my technical writing classes, a team of students, Laura Hart, Megan McCarty, Will Rogers, and Christopher Wood, was responsible for contributing to the Environmental Management System (EMS) plan for the Civil Engineering department at Clemson University. EMS plans for various departments had been requested by the classes' client, Clemson's Office of Environmental Health and Safety, and were needed in order to reduce the departments' environmental impact and demonstrate regulatory compliance. The team represented here inherited an EMS plan draft from a team in the previous semester's class and also inherited the team's name (Blazing Bridge Builders), a play on the Civil Engineering theme.

This mindmap, created with MindManager X5 Pro software, was one of the team's first attempts to gain a comprehensive understanding of the scope of their EMS project. Before creating the mindmap, the students had conducted research on the client's expectations, department's needs, and features of the genre of EMS plans. Their mindmap represents their view of the goals and tasks involved and, most importantly, the urgency or priority of those items. The first level of nodes on the map includes major parts of the EMS plan, as well as feedback goals and format concerns. The second level reflects goals within these categories. Finally, many of the goals branch into a third level: tasks necessary to complete the goals. The map reflects the team's questions as well as their answers. It also shows their developing understanding of the project, including its jargon, major players, and relationships among the complex network of tasks.

The team made visible its priorities for task completion. They used orange lines for tasks they thought they could reasonably complete during the current semester. But they also numbered the other tasks in descending order of priority, so that teams who followed them in future semesters could determine where to begin. And they used arrows to indicate that some lower-priority tasks are necessary precursors of higher-priority tasks, demonstrating that they were learning about the constraints of actual writing situations.

The mindmap is a fluid genre—it is created by rearranging words in a visual space. This map is one snapshot of the team's plans, which continued to evolve during the semester and remained a touchstone for the team as they worked. They used the map to check off tasks and left it behind for the next team who will pick up the project.

Summer Smith Taylor
English

Blazing Bridge Builders Mindmap

*Laura Hart, Megan McCarty,
Will Rogers, Christopher Wood*

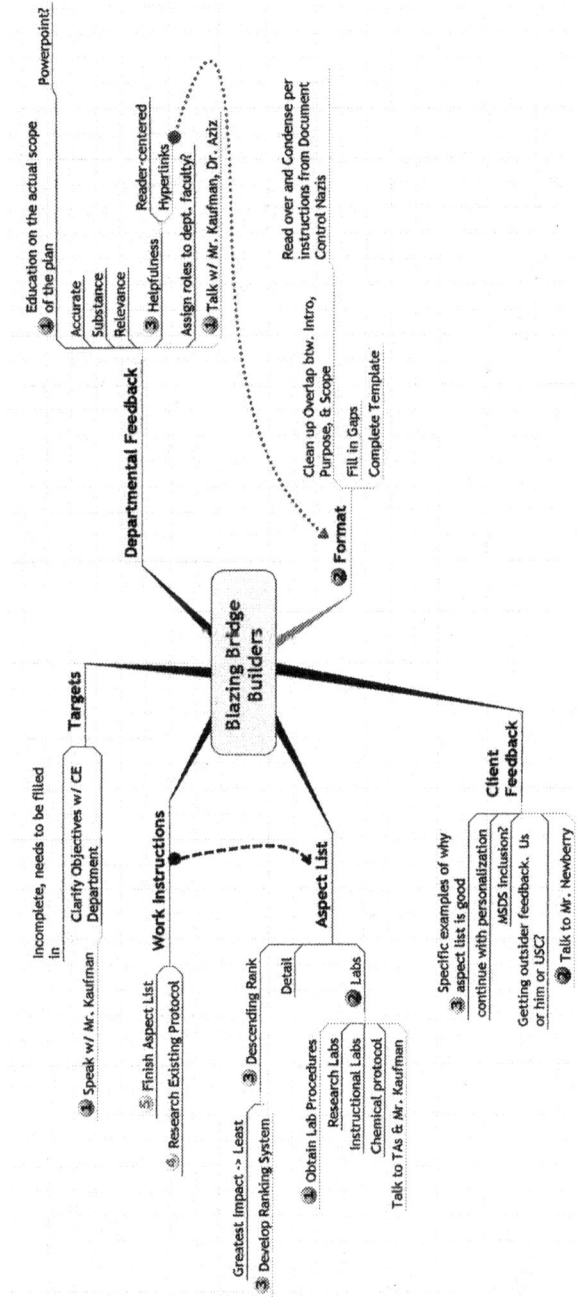

Civil Engineering

One of the cornerstones of engineering and the sciences are "Newton's three laws of motion" which specify how bodies behave when they experience a force. Students use them extensively. Despite this, I have been disappointed to realize that these "laws" are not well understood by many students. Consequently, about 15 years ago I began to force all the students to stand at the beginning of each class and recite in unison the three laws. I provided the wording in the syllabus, and then would simply say: "First Law! Second Law! Third Law!" Early on, there are always some smirks and eye-rolling but peer pressure helps force cooperation. After only a week or so, they have committed the laws to memory, and I can request that they say them out of order or that latecomers stand alone and recite them to the entire class. This process is also a good way to start class; it says, "We stand, say the laws, sit down, and then class begins."

I was asked to give a banquet speech at the American Society of Civil Engineers meeting attended by students, faculty, and practicing engineers. At the beginning I asked three faculty members to come to the front of the room and say the laws. After they mumbled for a bit with no laws forthcoming, I asked them to be seated and asked some of my students to come forward. They recited the laws with gusto and it was a great discussion point not only at the meeting that night, but around the department for the next several days.

I ask students to do a quick write about our Newton activity at the end of the semester, and Tarek Aziz's particularly engaged me because it showed that he (and Martin) had gone beyond the rote recital of the laws to an in-depth understanding of their larger meaning. They were truly beginning to know how the world works— an essential ingredient in the education of a successful engineer. In addition, this activity was the springboard to a voluntary discussion of a fundamental description of natural phenomena outside of class. Education at its best!

Ben Sill
Engineering

Reflection

Tarek Aziz

So we had to memorize these three laws, stand at the beginning of each class. "Paying Respect to Newton," he said. And we laughed and memorized our parts. Sure, I had heard them before, for brief moments during my undergraduate career. I knew that most of the stuff we used today was based on the assumption that Newton was telling the truth. Talk about trust. But it's a whole different game when have something stuck in your head. You begin to ask yourself, "What does that mean? Why are we saying this unabridged version of the laws?" Then, if you focus on it, you realize the answers are all around you. In three sentences Newton described how the world works. You begin to think that to really understand them you must make them a way of life.

Martin [a classmate] said to me the other day: "I was thinking about impact forces this morning. I think I figured it out." I replied "So, what'd you get?" And we proceeded into a thirty-minute discussion about what we thought an accurate means for determining impact forces was. We had both taken dynamics; we had heard the jargon, but it was when we stepped away from the cookie-cutter ideas and really thought about what governed the world that we really started to get somewhere. And we wrote a law of our own (or what we thought the law should be). We made up some variables, and then we sat and looked at the sheet of scrap paper and said: "That has to be it." As if we were discovering for the first time part of how the world worked. We then calculated how hard we would hit the ground if our parachute didn't open and shuddered when we saw the colossal number. What did we expect, a nice landing? We converted it into a strange equivalent, like vending machines. "That's about fifty of those," Martin said "stacked on top of each other." "It's a way of life, it really is." I said as I tossed the scrap paper into the trash. We now knew how impact forces worked; we had no need for our law.

First-Year English

As a graduate student and a first-time writing teacher, I knew I wanted to do more with reading and writing than the course syllabus suggested. Besides teaching my students how to effectively construct an argument, I wanted my students to play with language and explore its creative potential. I also wanted my students to meet and respond to Seamus Heaney, W.H. Auden, Adrienne Rich and Ron Rash. So near the end of a semester of writing academic arguments, I decided to include a day of poetry.

On the day of our discussion I had a cowboy poet, my friend Sam Renken, visit. Sam recited Shakespeare from the top of a desk, brought the words of Ginsberg to life, and showed my students that poetry can be, for lack of a better word, cool. He read some of his poetry, and explained "post-musheled goolashuralphanoliacan fluid," a term he coined where the last word in the line connects to the first word of the next line. Many of his poems utilize this technique, and he encouraged my students to think about things and make connections where they may not be so obvious.

As part of their final journal, my students had the choice to write a short story or a poem. Kevin Howell's, "My Post-Musheled Goolashuralphanoliacan Fluid Poem" was his attempt at Sam's technique, and I think it's excellent. He shows the inner workings of a college student ("good looking girls" are his "passion"), and every once in a while, drops in a reflection such as, "problems/ Only make someone stronger in life once they are overcome/ Adversity and you will succeed."

I was especially happy to read this poem because earlier in the semester Kevin had thrown away his copy of *Othello*. But his apparent ambivalence seems to vanish in his poem and provides an insight into his thoughts on our class, as he believes "emotional/Writings are the best because it is easy to identify with." Kevin's poem gives him a voice to express his thoughts, permission to play with sentence grammar, and a venue to create an emotional and relatable piece of writing. Like Sam's poetry, Kevin's poem helps to break down the alienating barriers the canon of poetry and the language of academic arguments often erect. As a result, he creates an accessible and playful reading experience for his classmates and me.

Skye Suttie
English

My Post-Musheled Goolashuralphanoliacan Fluid Poem

Kevin Howell

I like to read *Sports Illustrated* every Thursday
Is the fifth day of the week
Ends are a lot of fun because there is no class
Sucks, especially when there are no good looking girls
Are my passion in life
Is short so I think we need to make the most of it
Was a very beautiful day out today
I had a lot of fun because I ate at Pixie & Bills
From Buffalo are a pretty bad football team
Bonding is very important for being successful
Business people work very hard in life and rarely enjoy their earnings
Can be either monetary or emotional
Writings are the best because it is easy to identify with
A lot of money I would begin collecting cars
Are my second passion in life because I think they are incredible
Machines have helped our technology grow at an alarming rate
Of acceleration is 9.8 meters per second squared
Corners make any artwork more aesthetically pleasing
People is one of my biggest problems
Only make someone stronger in life once they are overcome
Adversity and you will succeed
With character because burning bridges can come back to haunt you
Should always love your parents because without them you wouldn't be
    here
Is where this poem about my views and thoughts is going to end

Anthropology-Study Abroad

Since 1999, colleagues and I have taken five student groups on Study Abroad trips to the Czech Republic—each time we visit Lidice, a village the Nazis obliterated in 1942. When visiting the site, students take photos, sit quietly on benches, and write in their journals. Silence envelops the group on the ride back to Prague.

Because Lidice is not a typical tourist destination, our Czech friends wonder why we Americans would choose to visit such a melancholy place. Amanda Gurganus' poem tells the tragic story of Lidice through the eyes of a little girl, as Amanda empathizes with the children who watched their fathers executed and their mothers and siblings exiled to concentration camps.

Through contrasting images, Amanda juxtaposes the serenity of girlhood with the horror of destruction and murder. On a "warm clear day," a man with a "spider strapped on his arm" invades the narrator's home. For no comprehendible reason, fumes enter the room "as cries become ghosts."

As an anthropologist, I continually teach the critical need for cross-cultural tolerance and understanding, but these often remain abstract concepts for students. But, when confronted directly by scenes of human struggles for freedom and justice, students more vividly grasp what we Americans often take for granted. Ghostly photographs in a museum, unfamiliar names on a wall, bronze statues in a park—the residents of Lidice begin as strangers to the American students, foreigners from another time and place. But during the visit and subsequent reflection, students empathize with the Lidice victims in a bond that unites all humanity. I want our visit to enlighten my students with an indelible lesson: that hope and understanding can conquer prejudice and tragedy.

John M. Coggeshall
Sociology

Remember Lidice

Amanda Gurganus

Learning how a young
woman should act, I help
my family how I can.
Woke up to a warm clear day
until the sun turned his head.

Our door shook from force,
a man with a black
four-legged spider strapped
on his arm. Mother shrieked

at the sight—Father ordered
us to get away, fast as we could.
We ran to the back door
into the barrel of a gun, held

by a cold face in a uniform.
Inside the house, mother pushed

up against a wall. Father fought
until he crashed to the floor.

Children everywhere driven
out of town, boys, girls,
baby Jaroslava clutched
in my arms. Brother Josef

clinging to my side. I do
not understand why
those men came, or what
we did wrong. As I sit

I count—eighty two
destined to die.
I sense fumes entering
the room—I listen
as cries become ghosts.

Truth in Song: American History, Our Oral Heritage

When I was in college studying music, relatives would ask me what I was going to fall back on. Hearing that question always angered me, because I translated it and heard what they were really saying: Music is insignificant.

Flash forward to a university professional development workshop. We are split into interdisciplinary groups and around we go introducing ourselves by discipline. Forging collaboration with a musician seems foreign to other faculty because in their fields, music is irrelevant.

History has always fascinated me, yet reading about events often felt impersonal; however I found something to grasp onto as I considered truths that lay embedded in songs sung by the people of different eras. Locked in these folksongs are images that I could see through the eyes of another. These ballads have life, conveying experiences, events, emotions and that is what I want to share with students. We study American history through these songs. The music is significant.

Then, the students reverse their roles in this oral tradition. The listeners become the creators of their own ballads to pass a story onto others. We delve into the Civil Rights era. They heard of the Birmingham church bombings. Their own ballads put them there. The music is relevant.

The untitled ballad by Laura Ogard lingers in my mind. It captures the innocence of a child, yet at the same time, conveys a great tragedy: indifference is as powerful as hatred. As the little one in the ballad forgets with sleep, we remember all the more.

Linda Dzuris
Performing Arts

106

Untitled

Laura Ogard

My momma told me today,
about this church downtown;
and how four little girls,
were killed underground.

Three were fourteen
and one was eleven;
seems kind of young,
to go to Heaven.

When my momma told me,
she didn't seem sad;
and my daddy even acted
a little bit glad.

So I asked my parents,
"Why aren't you crying?
isn't this sad,
these little girls dying?"

No answer I got,
to my childish imploring;
it seemed the whole issue,
they kept on ignoring.

"It doesn't seem fair,
that they should die so young;
when there are so many things,
they could've become."

Then my momma,
she held me close to her heart;
and my daddy he spoke,
a sad tale he did start.

"They're different than us,
our skins aren't the same,"
he seemed almost proud,
not one bit of shame.

"They were killed for no reason,
except that they were hated;
and us white people wish,
to stay segregated."

My little ears listened,
but my little heart didn't understand;
I thought we were free,
all across this land.

Later that night,
as I lay in bed;
thoughts of those girls,
ran through my head.

So from under the covers,
I began to crawl;
and ever so quietly,
crept down the hall.

With tears in my eyes,
I woke mom and dad;
and they looked at me funny,
like I had no need to be sad.

I protested, "Tell me!
I want to know why,
these girls can vanish,
with not as much as a sigh!"

The people that did this,
I thought were awful and mean,
for it was only the good life
they had ever seen.

I cried more and more,
for all the families with sorrow,
who would not have their daughters,
To kiss and hug tomorrow.

I hugged my parents,
and went back to my room,
praying the violence,
would be over soon.

As my head hit my pillow,
I thought of the blast,
the clock it struck twelve,
and it was now in the past.

Technical Writing

"Humor can be dissected as a frog can, but the thing dies in the process and the innards are discouraging to any but the pure scientific mind."

—E. B. White, *A Subtreasury of American Humor*

I should probably just accept E. B. White's insight about the conundrum inherent in the study of humor. An analysis of Katie Walter's poem will only result in the death of that which makes the poem funny. The innards, furthermore, are a bit discouraging: Katie and her classmates were adamant that chairman was a gender-neutral term.

Yet when I read her poem, I marveled at the way she engaged many of the things that we had discussed in class. Katie's approach to the assignment illustrates an art of the "contact zone." Contact zone pedagogy envisions the classroom as a space where people with differing opinions can interact. Open dialogue is supposed to foster mutual understanding, but I found that students usually already agreed with each other on most issues.

We have learned from studies of contact zone encounters, though, that those who are powerless often parody the ways of speaking or writing of those who are powerful. In giving my technical communication students a poetry-writing assignment, I had unintentionally created a contact zone. Poem after poem parodied my professorial discourse, using my own words (and editing marks) to poke fun at me, the individual who had the power to decide what counts as legitimate discourse. In effect, the poems became their counter discourse, and students comically raged against the conventions of professional communication, playing with generic expectations as illustrated by Katie's signing her poem as she would a letter.

Another poem demonstrated the consensus building that is supposed to happen in a contact zone. In a poem titled "Outside the Box," Jenny declared that she would not only think outside the box, she would "straddle the box like a whore." Her classmates cheered as I laughed.

Jenny then explained parenthetically that "whore" in the poem was a "rhetorical move designed to grab the reader's attention."

A rhetorical move designed to grab the reader's attention?

Where had she heard that before?

Joe Sample
English

110

Technical Writing

Katie Walters

why is it called Tech writing anyway?
i dont understand whats so technical,
there is are conventoins to every Genre,
Rules to every DISCOURSE!
Memos are so office space (ha ha)
A lot is where you park, not referring to many
Just in case you were wondering. (fragment)
It gets even more complicated that that.
(it mean rules, that referring to a lot)
Want me to advise you with some technical adice?
All right. (o no, not alright)
All together now, technical writing rules. Pun?
How about an allusion to the illusion to this mental delusion——supreme ELUSION!
can I compliment myself for the complement of poetry and choas?
Oh by the way, before you offer counsel to the council, you might ask the Chair.
Not chairman, what if it's a chick? Wait, i mean woman...
1 last thing...
watch for dangling modifiers, theyll get you every time.
And gerunds are verbs that end in-ing, dont forget that one,
Best of lucK getting technical,
At least in writing.
-technically yours-
katie walters

Secondary Content Area Reading

When my students and I began working with writing-to-learn strategies, their interest in the subject matter increased. Students were asked to capture the essence of an important idea in their discipline using cinquains. A cinquain is a five-line poem that does not rhyme, may be phrases or lists of words, and may simply provide more information with each line.

Directions for a Cinquain	Sample Cinquain
Line 1: a one word title	Cinquain
Line 2: two words describing the title	Five lines
Line 3: three words expressing an action	Does not rhyme
Line 4: four words expressing a feeling	Synthesize, integrate, connect, summarize
Line 5: synonym for the title	Poem

Darcy Coover's cinquain strips the concept of the Holocaust down to the essentials and provides connections between the World War II era and current events. Her use of "ethnic cleansing" and "genocide" with the terms "Holocaust" and "the final solution" created a connection between past and current events—something history teachers strive to accomplish. The fourth line ("death, sorrow, hate, fear") connects the actions and emotions of the Nazis and the Jews they persecuted and killed. Contrasting terms create a feeling of ambivalence. The elegant simplicity of Darcy's combination of words and phrases illustrates the power of poetry to bridge old and new events in history and to summon emotions that make events more memorable.

Heather Renzo, Dan McGlohorn, and Ryan Smith created a cinquain that summarizes an important American Civil War battle. They played with language until they captured the essential spirit and emotional cost of the battle of Gettysburg. This helped them connect emotionally with the concept and create a poem that summarized the battle's importance. Their phrase "Bloody battle" conveyed the horror of Gettysburg in understated terms. The phrase "Confederate high-water mark" created an illusion of an immense tide washing over everything, and then receding in the next line: "Ending of Confederate dreams."

In order to create a cinquain that succinctly conveys both the emotion and importance of an historical event, one must have in-depth knowledge of that event. Poetry can provoke deep and creative thinking about a discipline that is often reduced to isolated dates, names, and places. History really *lives* in these examples.

Victoria Gentry Ridgeway
Teacher Education

Holocaust

Darcy Coover

Holocaust
Ethnic cleansing
"the final solution"
death, sorrow, hate, fear
Genocide

Gettysburg

Heather Renzo, Dan McGlohorn, Ryan Smith

Gettysburg
Bloody battle
Confederate high-water mark
Ending of Confederate dreams
Pennsylvania

Art History

I teach art history to a variety of Clemson University students, ranging from first-year students hoping to major in Engineering to graduate students pursuing degrees in the Fine Arts. Most of the people who take my classes are undergraduate studio majors and their passion in life is to make art. When I was asked to participate in Clemson's Poetry Across the Curriculum initiative, I saw it as an opportunity to help these undergraduate studio majors connect to art's history through creation. In the course I teach on European and American Modernism, I asked my students to produce a work of art in writing. I gave them complete freedom, asking only that their poems be informed in some way by the visual art and poetry we studied. During the semester I read to my students work by poets who had relationships to the modern art movements we examined in class. They heard poems by Charles Baudelaire, Stéphane Mallarmé, Rainer Maria Rilke, Walt Whitman, Guillaume Apollinaire, Filippo Tommaso Marinetti, Richard Huelsenbeck, André Breton, and William Carlos Williams.

Elizabeth Schumpert's poem reflects the raw energy of modern visual and written art by intertwining the natural world with the man-made, and by interlacing rapture with violence. Like modern artists and poets, Elizabeth creates suggestive rather than descriptive images, and these images are shocking rather than pleasing. She makes comforting words frightening through unexpected juxtapositions ("velvet buttons" and "conjured army"), and heightens this disturbing effect by coining her own uncanny word: "fleshcoats." However, like the modern creators who preceded her, Elizabeth does not jolt her reader merely to provoke. Terms like "first shift," "members of the pack," and "masters' crutches" suggest that Elizabeth is evoking the complex experiences of soldiers or workers: people both energized and alienated by their labor. She captures perfectly one of the key conditions of modern life: the excitement and fear of living in a world where nature and people are bound within human institutions and their machinery. Elizabeth's poem moves me, because like the creative expression of many modern artists, it rages against "the machine."

Andrea Feeser

Art

First Shift

Elizabeth Schumpert

Sinewy, sexual
Melting in the heat.
Drizzling through the pores
of the cracked, leather tubing.
Encircling my thought,
An eagle emerges.
Wings shot with lightning,
It beats out elusive tufts
of disjointed rhythm,
Eating its heart out.
All members of the pack
Swarm the live fence.
Foaming and eager,
They finger the velvet buttons
of their conjured army.
Discovery:
The masters' crutches
are abundant in our fields.
Purchasing fleshcoats of downy dew,
Stretched, red vision aside,
They open the tiny mouths of dawn,
Making way for arrivals.

Landscape Architecture Design

This course was an experimental one. I was team teaching with a visiting artist, David Chamberlain. An accomplished sculptor, David had spent time in Japan studying calligraphy and haikus. Every weekend the students were asked to draw, to photograph, and to write a haiku—to present the same subject in three different forms. Because this was a required course in a professional degree program, it was risky to ask the students to explore other artistic means of expression or inspiration in the design studio. But here, Caroline Jones excelled. In three lines she summed up the story of her imaginary journey through the landscape. The first landscape architecture project was to be based on a narrative each student wrote. Caroline chose to write a haiku:

> The four friends depart,
> On a journey down rough roads—
> Higher now, they see.

From the narrative they generated, students were next asked to represent the journey as a three-dimensional model. Meanwhile, students practiced calligraphy with pen and ink, traced a journey in the palm of their hands, and sculpted a journey in sand. These were all explorations of the two-dimensional line, hoping to inform the three-dimensional line in the landscape, the path. When does it become place and when is it merely a means of moving through the landscape?

The final form of Caroline's project was a cardboard model of water carving out a path through a stone valley, and she was also able to convey the whole idea behind the journey in three lines. Although the exploratory drawings and models are wonderful and descriptive, it is the haiku, the poem, which arrives at a whole that is more than the sum of parts. By paring the narrative to its essence, Caroline succeeds in moving her audience to share the road she traveled.

Frances F. Chamberlain
Landscape Architecture

The Four Friends Depart
Caroline Jones

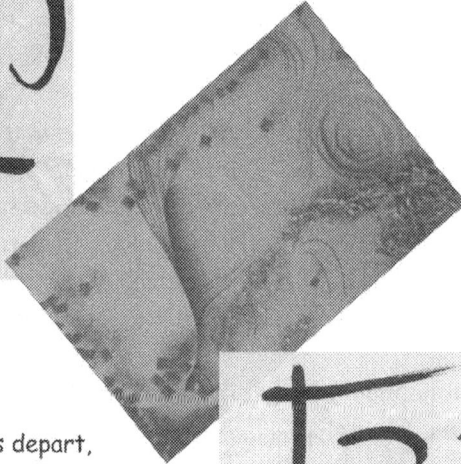

The four friends depart,

On a journey down rough roads -

Higher now, they see.

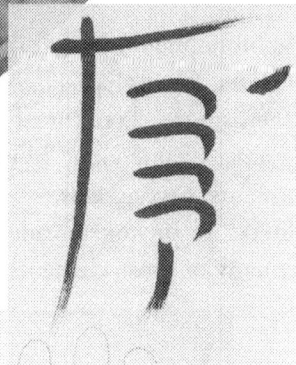

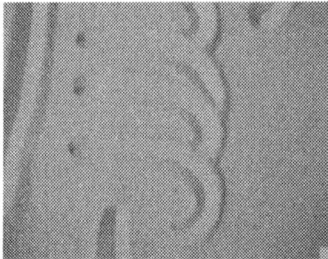

American Literature

Like most students in my honors section of American Literature, Meredith Allen is an overachiever. When I gave students a choice of two assignments regarding poetry across the curriculum—write a poem that takes a new approach to a subject directly from your major area of study, and/or write a poem that embraces any aspect of literature from a new vantage point—Meredith chose to do both, succeeding wonderfully in the process.

"Canta del Corazone" starts with onomatopoeia, then works with sound throughout, utilizing alliteration ("Release the pressure slightly,/allowing the soft, blue pipe to swell,") and sharp imagery to better understand and articulate the business of the heart. The biological terminology in particular helps make this poem feel authentic and real. I suspect that many of the jargon words ("saphenous" and "popliteal") were chosen for their sonorous qualities, as well their biological accuracy.

"Martyr of a Bibliophile" is a more traditional poem done in a traditional way—a love poem, of sorts. Words like "effervesces" and "crackling" help illuminate the way this speaker encounters literature. I particularly enjoy how Camus, Wiesel, and Lawrence "Beg not to flame alone." Literature provides sustenance and connects us beyond continents, beyond eras.

The best literature provokes readers to thought, feeling, and action. These poems capture many of those elements and ideas in vivid sparks of language that impress me still.

Ryan Van Cleave
English

Canta del Corazone

Meredith Allen

Lub dup lub dup
Cadence of your atria
And your ventricles;
Atrioventricular valve syllables,
The parting note of the semilunar
—And away stream your erythrocytes,
Hurrying, bouncing, stacking
As they surge along the subway.
Pause, press skin to bone with cold metal
Release the pressure slightly,
Allowing the soft, blue pipe to swell,
And listen for what Korotkoff heard.
Deep femur, saphenous, and popliteal reached
Return now, panting,
Straining against Newton,
Until your gasping breath is satisfied,
Touched by the pulmonary magic wand,
Changed from pumpkin to carriage yet again.
Surge forth once more; your 120 days are not yet passed.

Martyr of a Bibliophile

Meredith Allen

Glare, shimmering heat
The black shirt on my back burns;
My cheek is blushing under the sun's harsh gaze.
Walk the blinding walk,
Through the great solemn doors,
Down sediment step upon step
Into the cool, dim recesses.
Slowly the fire effervesces from my skin
And sparks the dusty volumes to life,
Crackling around me in my quiet corner.
Camus calls; Wiesel and Brother Lawrence
Beg not to flame alone,
And so I succumb to the yearning blaze.

Schooling as a Cultural Process

Much of what is happening in the world of public education today is driven by testing. Federal and state laws, many reflecting the "standards and accountability" movement, mandate tests that have implications for placement in learning groups, promotion from grade to grade, graduation from high school, admission to college, and even school funding. Students' academic lives are inundated with tests. Nonetheless, for as long as test performance data have been used for decision making, the practice has been criticized. What do tests, from IQ tests to standardized achievement tests to today's standards-based instruments, actually measure? Do they measure skills and dispositions that matter most in a student, or student recollection of algorithms, definitions, and facts set to memory? Do they reflect real-world situations, or are they artificial exercises? Does any one-shot administration reveal the actual learning and abilities of the student? Are tests even used correctly? Some states have used norm-referenced tests, those designed to measure student performance against other students by forcing scores into a normal distribution, as measures of achievement for promotion! And, of course, high stakes tests narrow curricula as teachers focus on that material for which they are held "accountable."

How many students (and their parents) conform to the system and allow test scores to shape their destinies? I am glad that Marla Kranick did not. If she had resigned herself to the arbitrary score assigned her, my life as a teacher would have been far less rich. This poem, an eloquent expression of Marla's rebellion against the test, suggests why.

Robert P. Green, Jr.
Teacher Education

I.Q.

Marla D. Kranick

If I were the sum of the score on your books
The quotient you applied to my supposed intelligence
I would have fulfilled your prophecy
And ventured no further than the lines
your hands had drawn

If I were the mere number your "standardized" score assigned me
Defined by the place where I fall within your percentile margin
I would have resigned myself to so little
And never discovered that my strengths
Lie in the very places
You dared me not to go

So . . . perhaps it is your questions that are too small
. . . or too square
. . . or too unimaginative
to contain the ambiguities
that make life the mystery that it is
and that make the philosophers question-askers
and the poets star-gazers
and the wise men wisdom-seekers

For they know that the complexity of life
Can rarely be contained in multiple-choice answers
or true and false questions
And so they dare to pursue the open-ended
And wait for the universe to answer back
But are not surprised
When it often does not

I am not the arbitrary score you assigned to me
I am not the sum of the questions I answered as you wished me to
For I am human
And, as such, nothing less than the handiwork of God
And the handiwork of God
Is complex and beautiful
In ways that you may never comprehend

Humanities

Providing students with a core of knowledge is one thing; engaging them with that knowledge is another. In my interdisciplinary humanities course, for example, the thirty-seven students represented a wide range of majors, backgrounds, and interests. As we began our study in the Italian Renaissance and headed toward the late twentieth century, the first challenge was to give the class an equal footing in art, architecture, literature, politics, history, and technology. Then the fun began! Using what I describe as a pedagogy of engagement, each large exam included a creative component which was handed in during the class period following the exam—a poem, greeting card, time capsule, or work of art. The results were immediate. The students came to feel a sense of ownership of the art or architectural work they used creatively in their projects and they learned from their classmates' work. Their own creativity also helped them become increasingly engaged with the material we were studying. This was reconfirmed by their final creative project, in which they were to choose any photograph of themselves and transform it technologically into an 8 x 10- or 9 x 12-inch Cubist, Futurist, Cubo-Futurist, or Expressionist self-portrait.

One of the most riveting of those remarkable thirty-seven, framed or matted self-portraits was the *Futurist Self-Portrait* by Bates Cagle, a graduating senior with a major in psychology and minor in sociology. About to begin her graduate studies in social work, but currently employed in a "data crunching" research project, Bates described herself as "very analytical," "not very creative at all." And she admitted that our class' creative components were "not something that came to me easily. I had to sit down and think about them." Despite such disclaimers, Bates' self-portrait says otherwise. Without prior artistic training, she transformed a picture of herself sitting in her favorite chair into the essence of the early twentieth-century Futurist style with all of its complex celebration of motion, technology, intensity, and spatial organization. And Bates did more: she captured the essence of creative engagement.

Alma Bennett
Humanities & English

Futurist Self-Portrait

Bates Cagle

General Chemistry

I have been a participant in communication-across-the-curriculum activities ever since the program's inception at Clemson. Yet I must admit to being a little dubious when the "poetry" program began. The course I was teaching at the time was a large lecture section of general chemistry, and although I had already implemented several writing assignments for these large classes, I was a little worried about how poetry would be received by students. In fact, I was so worried that I gave the class the option of writing either a short essay or a poem about chemical equilibrium. To my surprise over half the class chose the poem, and of those poems, a piece by Amy Williams is one of my all-time favorites.

The concept of chemical equilibrium is often hard for students to grasp. In normal usage the word "equilibrium" indicates a state of being at rest or at peace. In contrast, when used in chemistry the word denotes a state that is under continuous change, where forward and reverse processes occur at the same rate. To make matters worse, systems at equilibrium will change if the conditions are right, and students must not only be able to predict what will happen, they must also be able to calculate the results of the change. So, the topic of equilibrium, rather than giving students the serene peace that the name implies, actually gives students quite the opposite feeling. It is this horror that Amy captures so well in her poem "Chemical Equilibrium."

Not only does Amy get the chemistry right, indicating how the equilibrium constant K is calculated (if the products are large then K is large—or at least greater than one), she also includes the correct terminology (the principle of Le Chatelier) in a witty and charming poem. I'm afraid to say that I didn't even recognize Amy when she came forward to receive her prize for the best poem in the class (there were 199 other students). Indeed, if it were not for this unusual assignment I would certainly never have caught such a revealing glimpse of her creativity and conceptual understanding in this large and most technical of classes.

Melanie M. Cooper
Chemistry

Chemical Equilibrium

Amy Williams

Chemical equilibrium may be confusing to some
It may leave them frustrated and feeling quite glum.
Why can't a reaction just happen one way?
What's this Kw, Kc, and Ka?
If you'll sit back and listen, I'll show you the way
All you need is the principle of LeChatelier.
When you listen to him, it will help you decide
If the reaction will shift to the right or left side.
When the products are large, the reaction moves right
Don't let all the K business give you a fright.
When the products are many, K is greater than one
. . . Oh wait!! Please don't go—your lesson's not done.
When the reactants are large, K is smaller than one
And it's the left side this time that has all of the fun.
I can see you're not listening—you're bored as can be
So I hope on the test you improve on your D.